# DECODING
# HEALTH SIGNALS

# DECODING HEALTH SIGNALS

Silicon Valley's Consumer-First Approach
to a New Era of Health

## DR. JENNIFER SCHNEIDER

**L|A**  Lafayette American Publishing   Detroit, MI

# Contents

# *Acknowledgments*

IT ALWAYS TAKES A VILLAGE. At least in my case. And I am grateful to a number of people. Those who inspired me, those who taught me, those who helped me with this book, and the countless people who created space for me to pursue this endeavor.

A special thank you to my mom and dad; my brothers, Jamie and Jon; and Scott, Maggie, and Less for their ongoing support.

To the Livongo Team, current and past, for this opportunity we have created together. And in particular to Glen, Amar, and Lee for their comments and to my amazing coaching team, who gave me lots of material with which to work and inspired me every day through their interactions with our members.

And to the special Bean and Toby, Doug, Lauren, and Dougie for their tireless comments, revisions, and inspiration. There are many kinds of support . . . to Sara, Annie, Kelley, Susanna, Kristen, Seana, Caroline, Jess, and so many more for their friendship and patience.

And to my most treasured foxes, Fiona, Piper, and Angus, who give me the opportunity to be their mommy every day and amaze me

…with their endless wit, humor, energy, and love. To slightly modify the lyrics of a lovely song by Martina McBride:

In my children's eyes I am a hero
I am strong and wise and I know no fear
But the truth is plain to see
They were sent to rescue me
I see who I want to be
In my children's eyes

# About Livongo

IT'S IMPORTANT TO ACKNOWLEDGE the countless individuals, organizations, and companies that have selflessly dedicated themselves to helping others and saving lives, advancing science, medicine, and caregiving to a level that few dreamed of a hundred years ago. Because of their passion and efforts, we are living longer and dying of fewer causes than ever before.

Yet far, far more often than not, their achievements have come in spite of a healthcare system that has grown into a toxic maelstrom of complexity and confusion. Making matters worse, even with all this progress, Americans have fallen victim to a whole new subset of maladies like diabetes, heart disease, and obesity. The sad result is that chronic and mental health conditions are now the leading cause of death and disability in the country, accounting for 90% of the nation's $3.3 trillion in annual healthcare costs.[1,2]

---

1. Buttorff, C., Ruder, T. and Bauman, M. (2019). Multiple Chronic Conditions in America. [online] Rand.org. Available at: https://www.rand.org/pubs/tools/TL221.html.
2. "National Health Expenditure Data for 2016." CMS.gov, Centers for Medicare & Medicaid Services, 11 Dec. 2018, www.cms.gov/research-statistics-data-and-systems/statistics-trends-and-reports/nationalhealthexpenddata/nationalhealthaccountshistorical.html.

Of course, a trillion is an abstruse concept. How about we break it down? The average annual medical costs, per person, per year for Americans with:

- no chronic conditions (40%) are $8,500.[3]
- hypertension (39%)[4] are $11,800.[5]
- obesity (40%)[6] are $11,900.[7]
- prediabetes (33%)[8] are $15,000.[9]
- diabetes (7%)[8] are $19,500.[3]

These numbers are shocking and frustrating, no matter how you look at them. They are part of what motivated us to start Livongo. But what inspires us the most isn't numbers, but the people with chronic conditions whom our company was founded to empower, which is why we have created unique experiences for every member.

Our personalized approach provides members with the right information and support at the right time that leads to behavior change. We're accomplishing this with connected technology: cellular-enabled, bi-directional devices with over-the-air updates. We're also doing it through actionable, personalized, timely Health Signals, delivered through live coaching and shared digitally over devices, mobile apps, and our web portal. It's being done through Livongo's highly educated

x

[3.] "Economic Costs Of Diabetes In The U.S. In 2017". Vol 41, no. 5, 2018, pp. 917-928. *American Diabetes Association*, doi:10.2337/dci18-0007.
[4.] "Nearly Half Of U.S. Adults Could Now Be Classified With High Blood Pressure, Under New Definitions". *www.Heart.Org*, 2017, https://www.heart.org/en/news/2018/05/01/nearly-half-of-us-adults-could-now-be-classified-with-high-blood-pressure-under-new-definitions.
[5.] Wang, Guijing et al. "Annual Total Medical Expenditures Associated With Hypertension By Diabetes Status In U.S. Adults". *American Journal Of Preventive Medicine*, vol 53, no. 6, 2017, pp. S182-S189. Elsevier BV, doi:10.1016/j.amepre.2017.07.018.
[6.] Hales, Craig et al. "NCHS Data Briefs - Number 288 - October 2017". CDC.Gov, 2019, https://www.cdc.gov/nchs/products/databriefs/db288.htm.
[7.] Finkelstein, Eric A. et al. "Annual Medical Spending Attributable To Obesity: Payer-And Service-Specific Estimates". *Health Affairs*, vol 28, no. 5, 2009, pp. w822-w831. Health Affairs (Project Hope), doi:10.1377/hlthaff.28.5.w822.
[8.] "National Diabetes Statistics Report, 2017". Cdc.Gov, 2019, https://www.cdc.gov/diabetes/data/statistics-report/index.html.
[9.] Khan, Tamkeen et al. "Medical Care Expenditures For Individuals With Prediabetes: The Potential Cost Savings In Reducing The Risk Of Developing Diabetes". *Population Health Management*, vol 20, no. 5, 2017, pp. 389-396. Mary Ann Liebert Inc, doi:10.1089/pop.2016.0134.

expert coaches (following ADA, AADE, and AHA guidelines), who provide 24/7 live interventions and scheduled sessions. And we're achieving it with value drivers like closing gaps in care, medication optimization, and care coordination.

Best of all, Livongo is getting results. We're having a proven impact in terms of measurable clinical outcomes, where Livongo members have seen a 15% reduction in hypoglycemia,[10] systolic blood pressure reductions of 9mmHg,[11] 7.3% weight loss,[12] and a 74% Depression Score improvement.[13] We are leading the industry in satisfaction with a net promoter score of +64.[14] And we're demonstrating financial results, with cost savings of $108 PPPM.[15]

Industry-leading organizations are selecting and partnering with Livongo. We have a 95% retention rate with more than six hundred clients, representing 25% of Fortune 500 companies and more than twenty industries. We partner with fifteen of the largest health plans in the country and the top two pharmacy benefit managers (PBM).

And just as people are the reason Livongo exists, they're the reason we're succeeding. Our team's unparalleled expertise is what drives our strong growth. Livongo's leadership team is composed of executives with proven experience at well-known healthcare organizations, including Allscripts, Cerner, Castlight, Cigna, GE Healthcare, 23andMe, the American Diabetes Association, and Sanofi. And Livongo is leading the way in defining the future of healthcare and technology with the addition of executives from the technology industry, including Apple, Google, Intel, Oracle, Tesla, Twitter, and Evernote.

---

[10] Livongo Diabetes Book of Business. November 2018.
[11] Hypertension Beta Program Results. August 2018.
[12] Weight Management and DPP Book of Business. November 2018.
[13] Abhulimen, Sese, and Abigail Hirsch. "Quantifying The Economic Impact Of A Digital Self-Care Behavioral Health Platform On Missouri Medicaid Expenditures". Journal Of Medical Economics, vol 21, no. 11, 2018, pp. 1084-1090. Informa UK Limited, doi:10.1080/13696998.2018.1510834.
[14] Livongo Business Report. November 2018.
[15] Livongo Clients based on retrospective analysis of medical claims for clients with member populations that range from 3,000 to 100,000 covered lives. November 2018.

# *Preface*

THIS BOOK IS INTENDED TO INSPIRE YOU, the reader, to think differently about health and healthcare.

We tend to think of health as something that we exist with every day if we are taking care of ourselves. It's our optimal state of being. On the other end of the spectrum, we think of healthcare as the industry we turn to when we're sick. That's it, the two sides of the coin. It is a pretty simple delineation and, I would argue, one that ultimately has put too much burden on the healthcare industry. Today we can, in fact, all be much healthier, even those of us who struggle with chronic conditions, without having to turn to the healthcare industry.

The issue is that today's healthcare system fundamentally does not work for people with chronic conditions – we're unhappy, we're not getting healthier, and our costs keep escalating. And it seems the harder the system works to fix itself, the worse things get. Our current system was not designed to manage healthcare for people living with chronic conditions and yet (or maybe as proof), that is where the vast majority of the burdensome financial costs – and unsustainable levels of fiscal waste – come from. For the 180 million of us living with a chronic condition in the U.S., the whole thing is complex, confusing, and costly.[1]

But imagine if we could create an experience people actually loved. Imagine if we could truly empower people to improve their health and put them in charge of their own care. Imagine if we could reduce healthcare costs by 50%. This book is about a way to get there.

It is about the new category of companies arising to invent a better future and the challenges we have faced, the risks we have taken, and the successes we have achieved. It is about inspiring all of us to create something different.

My desire to completely reinvent the healthcare system as we know it is deep and personal. At our company, Livongo, we have already started down the path of this vision, but we still have a long way to go. So we invite everyone who shares our passion to join us. Together, we can empower more people to live better and healthier lives and at the same time reduce the snowballing costs of healthcare. Seems impossible, I know. But we are making it happen. Read on.

We know that new systems and technologies will be necessary to help those living with chronic conditions address their challenges, but technology alone will not be sufficient. We need new thinking and new approaches as well – a willingness to journey down paths that were previously unimaginable. Equally important, we need to retain the best part of our healthcare system – the highly trained, deeply committed, caring professionals. How do we put it all together so it's not even noisier for the people we're trying to serve?

As the visionary author William Gibson put it, "The future is already here, it's just not evenly distributed." We've started to build a healthcare experience for the whole person. One that scales down to a

---

1. Buttorff, Christine et al. Multiple Chronic Conditions In The United States. RAND Corporation, 2017.

very human level, democratizing solutions that have been inaccessible to most who need them. It will take innovative work to both improve clinical outcomes and drive down all these costs, but the answers are here. And they are here now. Once the scale of what's at stake is known, it's hard not to want to be part of the solution. So let's get started.

# INTRODUCTION

# *We Are What We Experience*

WE ALL HAVE OUR DATES. Those pivotal moments we remember with absolute clarity. The month, the day, the year. The exact location, the people we were with, even the weather. My first big one was January 12, 1987. I was a twelve-year-old girl sitting with my mom in my pediatrician's office. In the prior months, I had lost a ton of weight and could not seem to get enough to drink. I was so thirsty, I started bringing our big red Coleman water cooler jug to bed with me. Each night, I'd get up countless times to go to the bathroom.

I remember hearing my pediatrician repeatedly say the word DIE. But it had some other syllables attached to it that sounded like BEETEES. I had no idea what this word meant. But my mom took me straight to our local hospital, where I was admitted.

On January 12, 1987, I was diagnosed with type 1 diabetes. And as it does for so many others, this diagnosis changed my life. It changed the lives of my family as well. That day, I saw my father cry for the first time in my life. My dad, the second oldest of ten children, ran the family business. He had always been a rock, capably and confidently providing for everyone. Until that day, I had never seen him vulnerable. Over time, I came to understand that he felt guilty for my diagnosis, and all that came with it – a life-or-death dependence on injected insulin, risks of developing heart disease, blindness, kidney failure and other complications of type 1 diabetes. As a parent, he was bothered by a conviction that he had somehow passed along some bad bit of genetics and was responsible for my diagnosis. He wanted to own that responsibility. To take it away from me. He repeatedly wished that he could shoulder this diagnosis for me. For all of us, it was a sudden turn, an unexpected detour on a journey that had been a relatively straight shot until then. But it was not a stop sign.

In so many ways, I was a lucky kid, more fortunate than most. I was born into an amazing family. We were solidly middle class, so we had access to care and lived near one of the nation's finest medical institutions. Dr. Roger Nelson, an endocrinologist at the Mayo Clinic and an incredible physician, was instrumental in giving me the tools I needed to face my new condition. He started with the clinical parts that were critical for me to know for day-to-day survival. But more importantly, he taught me the behavioral strengths I would need for the long haul of this condition. From the beginning, he treated me like a person first and a person living with a medical condition second. While advocacy groups in diabetes are credited with attempting to change the nomenclature from "diabetic" to "person with diabetes," Dr. Nelson did this for me long before it became common practice. As hard as my dad struggled to bear the burden of living with diabetes for me, he understood that he could not. Diabetes, as we all quickly realized, was something that I would live with every second of every day of my life until there was a cure. At age twelve, I had a new job: to manage my diabetes. And my mom and dad did the most important thing they could for me: They empowered me with tools and confidence and surrounded me with experts who would teach me to excel at my new job. From the very first day of my diagnosis, it was clear that this was "my thing." I sincerely believe that their approach of putting me in charge made me stronger and the disease less overwhelming. This was one of the many gifts that my parents gave me as I began to work my way through the quagmire that is life with diabetes.

Every person diagnosed with diabetes deals with it in their own way. For some, it's paralyzing and emotionally debilitating because every activity, every food choice, every nuance outside of a predictable pattern means you have to alter or adjust your medications, food, and activity in real time, just to stay safe. Many people and family members live in a constant state of fear about inadvertently going off the rails and hitting dangerous blood glucose levels. Fortunately for me, being diagnosed with diabetes turned out to be incredibly motivating. I was determined to manage diabetes within the context of who I was, a seventh-grader on the brink of puberty. Somehow, I knew I would have to do this to succeed. Maybe my

• • •

**At age twelve, I had a new job: to manage my diabetes.**

• • •

parents and doctors knew this too, perhaps explaining why I was granted permission for a two-hour leave from the hospital just four days after my diagnosis to attend my middle-school dance. Yes, I wore the hospital ID band, but my best friend, Jessy, brought me a long-sleeved pink shirt and I tucked the band inside it. As I shared my news with Jessy, I made her promise not to tell our friends. From the outset, I made sure it was me, not my parents, not Dr. Nelson, who was in the driver's seat. This was my news to share and my condition to control.

Although I could not articulate it at the time, this idea of *empowerment* – especially for someone who has to live with a new medical truth about themselves every day, without ever taking a break – was critical to my understanding of managing chronic conditions. Chronic conditions can be lonely, isolating, anxiety-ridden, and incredibly frightening. The more we know about our condition and the better we understand our own health, the less scary it becomes and the more confident and capable we grow. To successfully empower, there needs to be an environment (like the one my parents created for me) that provides the person with a chronic condition with constant motivations and expert insights on the specific skills and tasks at exactly the right time.

I am constantly inspired by people with type 1 diabetes. Nicole Johnson became Miss America while openly wearing an insulin pump during her swimsuit competition. Jay Hewitt raced for the U.S. national triathlon team. Like them, I worked through the newly imposed necessities of managing my condition while simultaneously developing a healthy disrespect for every "you can't" or "you shouldn't" that came my way. I lied about having type 1 diabetes and went scuba diving, climbed Mount Kilimanjaro, and ran a marathon. I have

. . .

**I credit my parents and my diabetes for my underlying belief that anything is possible.**

. . .

continually reacted to life with diabetes like a water balloon. Whenever I've been squeezed in one place (restrictions placed on my eating and needing regular medications), I've expanded in others (greater physical and mental challenges). I credit my parents and my diabetes for my underlying belief that anything is possible.

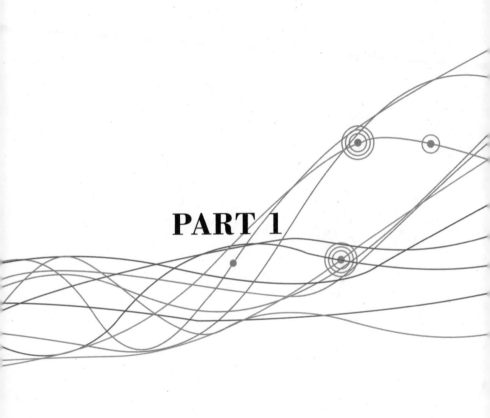

# PART 1

# CHAPTER 1

# *The Great Obstacles*

I WOULD NEVER WANT TO IMPLY that managing a chronic condition is easy. Quite the contrary. There's a long list of tasks to complete every single day. For those of us living with a chronic condition, a large percentage of our cognitive overhead is dedicated to this job full time. I am constantly scanning, planning, plotting. "Are there fast-acting carbohydrates nearby if I go low?" "Do I have my insulin packed?" If I want to go for a run, I need to identify the time to do it and remember to ramp down my meds. Unless you live day-to-day with a chronic condition, it is nearly impossible to truly understand. It's like parenting – you cannot completely imagine what it is like until you actually become one. One of my college hall mates, Beth Hantman (née Bowman), with whom I drove across the country, contacted me recently when her nine-year-old daughter, Hazel, was diagnosed with type 1 diabetes. Beth was emotional on the phone, saying, "I had no idea that you did all of this." I didn't want to explain to her why she didn't know. Most people don't know. Because people with diabetes rarely call attention to their condition.

9

Either they don't want to be labeled or singled out as different, or they fear the stigma that might be attached. As adults, it can grow even worse — they might fear discrimination at work, or loss of insurance benefits or coverage.

They may be anxious about enduring the awkward silences — or the even more awkward exchanges — that often follow the news. Many people understand, of course. But even people familiar with the condition can still be unsure how to talk about it with someone who has diabetes. Whether the conversations begin benignly ("I'm so sorry") or blithely ("Wow. So what's wrong with you?"), there's a consistent undertone — even with the best of intentions — that singles out people with diabetes, reminding them of something that they already know all too well. This unintentional marginalization is quite real and needs our attention before it becomes even more serious. For all these reasons and more, those of us with diabetes, generally, tend to be quiet about it.

• • •

**It's an endless array of incommensurable objects with competing and overlapping systems, formats, agendas, and tools.**

• • •

Unfortunately for us, we're the only ones who are quiet. Everything else is loud. First, there are all the choices. For those of us who just want to be healthy again, the healthcare system has generated so many things to "help" us: devices, guidance, apps, medicine, and appointments. It's an endless array of incommensurable objects with competing and overlapping systems, formats, agendas, and tools. At Livongo, we call this the Myth of More.™ It's like a parent who can't calm a toddler so instead throws every single squeaky stuffed animal and talking doll into the crib in a desperate attempt to solve the problem. But, of course, the problem is not being solved. Instead, more often than not,

10

more choices leads to confusion, complexity, and cost – what we call the three Cs. The market is filled with so many recommendations, experts, and systems that it can be overwhelming for those of us with chronic conditions. We are often left not really understanding what to do or when to do it. Even worse, the "help" given to us is often conflicting, and systems "designed" to make things easier create hardship instead. In the end, we can be left with an underlying distrust about which device, expert, or approach will even be useful. In our current healthcare model, while trying to empower people to better manage their conditions, we've actually created a system that winds up doing just the opposite.

One of the worst parts of all is that, for people with chronic conditions, there is often a haunting feeling that we are the ones who are somehow responsible – and if we were only smarter, more organized, more methodical in our approach, the system would work just fine. But I have experienced, firsthand, how upended things can get. As a doctor and the president of a company that empowers people with chronic conditions to live better and healthier lives, one might assume I have a leg up or know a good workaround to keep those three Cs – confusion, complexity, and cost – from encroaching on the lives of people with chronic conditions. But no one is immune and I have not been spared. Even with my degrees, training, and experience – not to mention access to the best resources available – I have stumbled over the complexity, become mired in the confusion, and watched slack jawed as costs piled up that were entirely avoidable. It's all a jumble, honestly, with complexity leading to confusion and compounding each other, ultimately resulting in increased cost. Let me give you an example of how each of the three Cs affects us, and more specifically how each has affected me.

## *Confusion*

This confusion starts after diagnosis, when we simply do not understand what happened or know where to start. After that, every meal is a challenge: Can I eat this? What is right for me? Perhaps we are told to measure our blood pressure but, okay, what's next? How often? What do I look for? Should I worry? How much should I worry? What do I do with the information? These thoughts alone are enough to make your blood pressure rise.

There may be no clearer or more relatable example of confusion than prescription medications. I'm not talking about the labels on the bottle, but rather the reams of supplemental instructions and warnings that come with even the most basic medications, which can be as verbose and confusing as the user agreement for a cell phone contract. Research indicates most people don't even read them because of the confusing jargon, tiny type, and user-unfriendly design. As one FDA spokesperson summed it up in 2011, "By objective measures, current systems for providing high-quality, easily accessible prescription medication information to patients have failed."[1] Consider the number of medications someone with a chronic condition has, and you can begin to sense the scale of the problem.

That confusion engulfs every aspect of healthcare. Speaking as an experienced medical professional who's lived with diabetes for more than thirty years and has learned to navigate the system with the best of them, even I feel engulfed by the confusion at times.

A few years ago, with the belief that anything is possible, I decided to enter the Ironman Santa Rosa triathlon. To the casual observer, a triathlon is a combination of three continuous races: swimming, cycling, and running. But for triathletes, there is a another equally

---

[1] "Prescription Labels And Drug Safety: Can You Read this Drug Label?". Consumer Reports, 2011, https://www.consumerreports.org/cro/2011/06/can-you-read-this-drug-label/index.htm.

important race involved: managing one's equipment. Transitioning from one leg to the next is a sport in itself that not only adds precious minutes to your overall time, but can be a stressful experience, especially when things go wrong. It requires organization, preparation, and practice to go smoothly. There's the wetsuit, bike, shoes, tape, food, water, ointment (don't ask) – it's not unlike all the paraphernalia people with chronic conditions have to manage every single day.

And in my case, some of that was included, too. Race officials instructed me to check in my insulin pump at the medical tent, away from my equipment and against my better judgment, but I placed my faith in their system and jumped into the Russian River. After emerging from the 2.4-mile swim and ready for the 112-mile bicycle ride, I was stopped cold in my tracks. My insulin pump was not at the medical tent and none of the medical personnel knew where it was. While my competitors quickly changed and hopped on their bikes, eating and drinking while underway, I needed to constantly track my blood glucose and adjust my insulin accordingly using my pump. My first thought was, "Great, not only will I not finish the Ironman, but I'm going to land in the hospital, too." When the race medics finally found a pump, it wasn't even mine, but another racer's. This only compounded the issue – what was that other poor soul experiencing?

Eventually they located my pump, but I was furious. Looking back, it occurred to me that negotiating the chaos of the triathlon transition stations (equipment and all) was eerily analogous to the confusion of the healthcare system (though much louder and sweatier). Tracking down a pharmacy to fill a prescription, deciphering an insurance billing statement, having your call transferred a dozen times before finding the right person to talk to (and the hours spent waiting on hold) – an enormous part of keeping yourself healthy has little to do with caring for your health and is more about figuring out the

13

way things work. Managing a chronic condition takes enough effort as it is, but in a system as disorganized and mystifying as the world of healthcare, it's often the easier part.

Very much like the disorganization that turned my triathlon from a challenge into an ordeal, streamlined systems purportedly intended to assist people with medical care often just increase the confusion and stress. The extra time and effort required of us makes the process more difficult for everyone and even, tragically, unmanageable for some.

## Complexity

Then there's complexity, the Byzantine trials involved in following all of those new regimens and navigating the various instructions and billing systems and "innovative" technologies that "might" be complementary (but usually aren't). We may have one specialist looking at our diabetes. Another at our heart. And a third one giving us advice on muscle pain. Ping-ponging from issue to issue, doctor to doctor, leaves us frustrated, anxious, and isolated. So many experts, so little clarity.

One in four Americans have multiple chronic conditions,[2] becoming three in four over the age of 65.[3] Then consider that for each additional chronic condition, the complications and costs associated with it double,[4] so that treating a patient with four conditions requires up to sixteen times the effort and resources of treating those with one. That's not just a math word problem, it's a societal problem. A startlingly complex one that leaves a lot of room for error. And one

[2] Parekh, Anand K. et al. "Managing Multiple Chronic Conditions: A Strategic Framework For Improving Health Outcomes And Quality Of Life". Public Health Reports, vol 126, no. 4, 2011, pp. 460-471. SAGE Publications, doi:10.1177/003335491112600403.

[3] Gerteis, Jessie et al. Multiple Chronic Conditions Chartbook. U.S. Department Of Health And Human Services - AHRQ, 2010, https://www.ahrq.gov/sites/default/files/wysiwyg/professionals/prevention-chronic-care/decision/mcc/mcccha-rtbook.pdf.

[4] Adler-Waxman, Amalia. "This Is The Biggest Challenge To Our Health". World Economic Forum, 2017, https://www.weforum.org/agenda/2017/12/healthcare-future-multiple-chronic-disease-ncd/.

that needs to be fixed, now.

Not long after I was hired at Livongo, I went to Indianapolis to tour the Lilly headquarters, the world's largest manufacturer of insulin. It was an inspiring visit. The Lilly executives showed us really cool, innovative products they were building to help people on insulin. In my excitement to explore what they were creating and hold the products up to my body, I did something I very rarely do: I detached my insulin pump. When I got back to my hotel, I realized I had left my pump at Lilly. I called their offices, but no one could find it. Once again, my pump was nowhere to be found.

I take short-acting insulin, which means that I can be off my pump for only an hour or two at a time. After that, my blood glucose increases rapidly and it becomes a medical emergency. Predictably, it started to climb, quickly getting in the 400- to 500-range (80 to 120 mg/dL is normal). This is a point when a person with diabetes can no longer make clear decisions and their situation becomes dangerous. When people who are dependent on medication cannot access it, the system breaks down pretty rapidly.

So there I was, alone and in serious need of insulin but unable to get it, looking out my hotel room window at Lilly headquarters, the global center for insulin and a veritable Willy Wonka factory of shiny new diabetes medications and products. It was almost too literal to be a metaphor. The help I needed was right in front of me, yet beyond my grasp because of forces out of my control. Fortunately, because I'm a physician, I was able to get a new prescription written right away. Most people are not as lucky as I was.

Millions of people living with chronic conditions regularly experience similar predicaments – but whereas my situation was absurdly simplistic, theirs are typically very complicated. In fact, complexity itself is one of the main obstacles between most patients and

15

the care they need. It's difficult enough getting through the healthcare gauntlet in the best of times, but during an emergency or for an unscheduled need, it can seem impossible.

The healthcare system is a labyrinth of protocols, a Gordian knot of siloed institutions each speaking its own language and operating on a different frequency. It forces laymen to be their own medical Sherpa, transporting lab results across town, translating incompatible billing systems, traversing an unfamiliar, convoluted landscape of corporate bureaucracy, often times completely on their own.

And it can have serious results. Unweaving the tangled web of healthcare is a part-time job for those with chronic conditions. And low-income patients who don't have the luxury to wait on the phone for hours to get a prescription, or are forced to stretch the supply of their medication because of rising costs, often have to choose which job is more important: working to be healthy or working to survive. A grim substantiation: It's estimated that as many as half of all chronic condition treatment failures in the U.S. – including 125,000 deaths a year – can be attributed to people not taking their medication the way it was prescribed.[5]

I passionately believe that no one should feel physically threatened by the failure of a system when solutions are as close to them as that building was to me.

## Cost

Then there's the final C: cost. Chronic conditions account for 90% of all healthcare costs. Insulin and related medications are, of course, notoriously expensive. Then there is the constant cost of blood glucose test strips and continuous glucose monitors that help you stay on top of the condition. Then there are the standard costs that

[5] Benjamin, Regina M. "Medication Adherence: Helping Patients Take Their Medicines As Directed". Public Health Reports, vol 127, no. 1, 2012, pp. 2-3. SAGE Publications, doi:10.1177/003335491212700102.

come with simply seeing your doctor. Add to that any ER visits or urgent-care costs from complications that arise when your doctor isn't available (chronic conditions have an inconvenient way of flaring up during nonbusiness hours). None of these costs are trending down. Between 2002 and 2013, the cost of insulin more than tripled – from $231 to $736 a year per patient.[6] People with diabetes are endlessly thinking, "How are we supposed to budget for this? How are we even going to pay for it?" One phrase we hear a lot, "I don't want to have to mortgage my house." They might go off of their insulin or skip therapy appointments because the bills are just too high. According to a recent Yale study,[7] one in four people with diabetes have skimped on insulin because of the high costs.

There's an emotional cost to this: People feel frightened, guilty, shameful, or depressed. Or they wallow in *just-ignore-it-and-maybe-it-will-go-away* mode. The problem is, of course, these feelings and behaviors often put them in real danger.

Yep, I have a story about this one, too. A couple months after the birth of my third child, I returned to my job at a company that was prepping for an initial public offering. Between the stresses of work and caring for my three-year-old, two-year-old, and my nursing newborn, I was extremely tired. So I turned off the alarms on my continuous glucose monitor (CGM) in the hope of getting a wee bit of sleep undisturbed by its beeping. A few hours later, I awoke in my bedroom surrounded by paramedics asking me questions. For a brief and horrifying moment, I thought I'd had a stroke. I could neither move my limbs nor speak. The emergency medical technicians gave me a big shot of sugar, and as soon as it entered my bloodstream, I felt better. It turned out I'd had a nasty bout of very low blood glucose, what in medical lingo we call hypoglycemia. But the real irony was

[6] Hua, Xinyang et al. "Expenditures And Prices Of Antihyperglycemic Medications In The United States: 2002-2013". JAMA, vol 315, no. 13, 2016, p. 1400. American Medical Association (AMA), doi:10.1001/jama.2016.0126.
[7] Herkert, Darby et al. "Cost-Related Insulin Underuse Among Patients With Diabetes". JAMA Internal Medicine, vol 179, no. 1, 2018, p. 112. American Medical Association (AMA), doi:10.1001/jamainternmed.2018.5008.

that I had all the latest and greatest medical gear and it *still* happened. I was using an insulin pump and a CGM, which sent its data to my pump. My data was right there showing that my blood glucose had plummeted. Despite the clear message of what was happening, there was no intervention, and no alarm, since I had turned it off.

Later, I totaled the actual price of this event, in dollars. Including the cost of the CGM (an out-of-pocket expense because my insurance carrier at the time wouldn't cover it), my insulin pump (which was covered), the ambulance ride, and the EMT visit, the grand accounting came to $52,000.

You might be saying to yourself, "But this whole thing was your fault. You turned off the alarm. You created the problem and caused the additional costs." This is precisely the point. I am a doctor. I was working at a healthcare technology company. And I am human. Here's the thing about people with chronic conditions: We never get a day off. Not one. To expect 24/7 perfection in self-management is simply not realistic.

In some ways, it's even harder to stay vigilant when you have type 2 diabetes. The good news about type 2 is that it's often quite possible to control the condition through diet and lifestyle changes. But as Dr. Bill Polonsky, an expert on diabetes burnout, has pointed out in a recent interview, it's hard to stay motivated when your only motivation is having things stay pretty much where they are right now. For most people, that's not a great motivator.

Diabetes is a condition where the doctor says, "Hey, Joe, listen, if you can take the following medications, improve your life with what you're eating and how you're exercising, try to be vigilant and lose a little weight, and just stay on track every day for the next ten, twenty, thirty, forty years, here's what's in it for you, here's what's most likely to happen...nothing." In other words, no catastrophic illness, no organ failure, no heart conditions, none of the things that people with diabetes are at increased risk of suffering. As Dr. Polonsky points out, it's hard to stay motivated when the only reward is nothing. Why fill your life with confusion for that?

I offer these stories because I hope they will help you understand what it is like to live with a chronic condition. It is hard work. Every day. And it is why I am so passionate about my job – building meaningful products to make day-to-day living with a chronic condition easier. But this is not about me. I will be okay. It is about millions of other people who have similar hard work to do with fewer resources. This passion is shared by my colleagues at Livongo. I don't mean this rhetorically. In fact, more than a third of Livongo employees live with a chronic condition, and another third have a family member who lives with one. One of my firm beliefs is that to solve a problem you have to deeply understand it. The Livongo team does: Our team includes sons who have grown up watching their dads struggle with diabetes management who now must navigate the system to get dialysis for diabetes-related kidney failure. We are also parents who have gained weight as we have gotten older, seen our blood pressures rise, and are now working hard to drop our weight and control our blood pressure. We are brothers who have suffered with depression. And daughters who once sat in a doctor's office and were told that our lives would never be the same.

**• • •**

**Our mission drives us to transform the three Cs in every member's life.**

**• • •**

As I point out throughout this book, I have tremendous respect for the medical industry, the doctors and nurses who have spent years learning how to manage acute care and other illnesses. Our current medical system is unparalleled, should you require acute care. However, chronic care needs another solution. A healthier solution. And so at Livongo, we set out to do something different: to start with diabetes and expand into caring for the whole person. Our empathetic tools offer up actionable information at the right time in the right way, delivering curated choices that don't overwhelm but instead encourage and inspire.

We are on a mission to empower people who, like us, have chronic conditions and want to live better and healthier lives, allowing them to enjoy their jobs, their families, and their friends. Our mission drives us to transform the three Cs in every member's life, ultimately turning confusion into clarity, complexity into simplicity, and cost into affordability.

## *Chapter One Summary: The Great Obstacles*

- The devices, guidance, apps, medicine, and appointments created by the healthcare system to "help" us actually overwhelm those with chronic conditions. We call this the Myth of More.

- More choices leads to the three Cs: confusion, complexity, and cost.

- As Livongo creates a new system of health, we work to turn confusion into clarity, complexity into simplicity, and cost into affordability, empowering people to live better, healthier lives.

# CHAPTER 2

## *Creating the Map*

LET'S START WITH A STUNNING FACT: Care for chronic conditions is responsible for 90% of U.S. healthcare costs.[1] Yet chronic conditions are very rarely in the spotlight, which is surprising if you consider this comparison: Fewer than 13,000 people have died from Ebola since the virus was first identified in 1976.[2] That means a disease most of the world knows of has killed fewer people than the population of Brecksville, Ohio (a town few people outside of Ohio have ever heard of). Today, in the U.S. alone, more than 180 million people live with chronic conditions.[3] If they were to form their own nation, it would be the world's ninth-most-populous country, just ahead of Russia. It's understandable that the press would give more coverage to the outbreak of a virus, but the disproportionate scale of the attention does demonstrate how completely chronic conditions are ignored.

These chronic conditions include diabetes, hypertension, hypercholesterolemia, asthma, and behavioral health (such as depression, anxiety,

---

[1] (Buttorff et al.)
[2] "Ebola Virus Disease Distribution Map". Centers for Disease Control and Prevention, cdc.gov, 2019, https://www.cdc.gov/vhf/ebola/history/distribution-map.html.
[3] (Rand, 2017)

sleep disorders, and substance abuse). To complicate matters, it's rare that one condition exists without a second or third. Up to 71% of people with diabetes also have hypertension.[4] Approximately 90% of people with type 2 diabetes are overweight.[5] More than one-third of people with diabetes suffer from depression, and nearly 12% have major depression.[6] The challenge with multiple chronic conditions is that they inevitably spiral out of control. For example, depression leads to poor adherence to lifestyle changes and medication schedules, which leads to poor glycemic control, greater health issues, and higher health costs. It's a double-edged sword: People with diabetes are more likely to have depression, and people who are depressed are more likely to develop diabetes.[7]

• • •

**Care for chronic conditions is responsible for 90% of U.S. healthcare costs.**

• • •

In 2016, diabetes was the seventh-leading cause of death worldwide,[8] with an estimated 1.6 million deaths directly caused by diabetes.[9] An estimated 17.9 million people died from cardiovascular diseases,[10] which more often than not, coexists with diabetes. Those are pretty alarming statistics, and these are numbers that demand action.

But even more alarming is the underreporting of the statistics in areas where there is simply no funding available for treating the condition. When I was in medical school, I spent time at Dhaka Shishu Hospital in Bangladesh helping to build an informatics system so that they could better track what came into their emergency room. At Dhaka Shishu, the children's hospital ("*shishu*" means "children" in Bengali),

[4] (Wang et al.)
[5] "Obesity And Overweight Fact Sheet". Who.Int, 2013, https://www.who.int/dietphysicalactivity/media/en/gsfs_obesity.pdf.
[6] Andreoulakis, E et al. "Depression in diabetes mellitus: a comprehensive review." *Hippokratia* Vol. 16, 3, 2012, pp. 205-214.
[7] Smith, Kathleen. "Diabetes and Depression: Managing Your Mental Health." PsyCom.net, 25 Nov. 2018, www.psycom.net/depression-and-diabetes.
[8] Stokes A, Preston SH. "Deaths Attributable to Diabetes in the United States: Comparison of Data Sources and Estimation Approaches." *PLoS ONE* 12(1): e0170219, https://doi.org/10.1371/journal.pone.0170219
[9] "Diabetes: Key Facts." World Health Organization, 30 Oct. 2013, www.who.int/news-room/fact-sheets/detail/diabetes.
[10] "Cardiovascular Diseases (CVDs)." *World Health Organization*, World Health Organization, 17 May 2017, www.who.int/news-room/fact-sheets/detail/cardiovascular-diseases-(cvds).

the head of the emergency room informed me that they had never seen a case of type 1 diabetes. I was understandably surprised. But someone soon told me the reason: "We never diagnose something we cannot treat – and insulin is simply too expensive." Out of the 425 million adults (between the ages of twenty and seventy-nine) with diabetes globally, about one-half of them have not been diagnosed and, consequently, have no idea that they are living with the condition.[11]

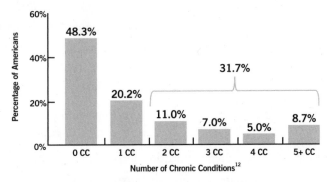

Source: AHRQ Multiple Chronic Conditions Chartbook, 2010

The costs of treating diabetes are escalating for everyone involved. Healthcare providers have to balance limited resources with increasingly higher demands. People who have diabetes and hypertension have average annual medical costs of around $13,700.[13] But employer-sponsored benefits wind up impacting everyone, as workers without chronic conditions – whose annual medical costs average less than $6,000 – wind up covering more of the tab as deductibles and copays rise. All of this adds to increased economic hardships that our overall enconomy is finding increasingly difficult to absorb.

To put it simply, chronic conditions are an increasingly heavy burden on individuals and families, workplaces, the healthcare system, and society at large. One can drown in the numbers (and people often

[11] International Diabetes Federation. IDF Diabetes Atlas, 8th edn. Brussels, Belgium.2017, http://www.diabetesatlas.org.
[12] (Gerteis et al.)
[13] "Economic Costs Of Diabetes In The U.S. In 2017". Vol 41, no. 5, 2018, pp. 917-928. American Diabetes Association, doi:10.2337/dci18-0007.

do – chronic conditions account for a third of all medical debt,[14] the leading cause of bankruptcy for consumers in the U.S.[15]). In 2017, the cost to our healthcare system of treating those with type 1 and type 2 diabetes was $237 billion.[16] For hypertension, the latest costs were $51 billion.[17] And heart disease and stroke – which people with diabetes are two times more likely to suffer[18] – cost the healthcare system another $199 billion.[19] Across all chronic conditions, the spend adds up to more than $1 trillion, putting an enormous drag on the overall economy. If we can reduce those expenses by, say, 10%, that's $100 billion poured back into our economy. Think about it, 3% of that trillion could pay for universal pre-K in our country, and 6% would pay for free college education for all our kids. Bottom line: Fixing this enormous burden from our current healthcare costs could have amazingly positive benefits to our country's long-term financial viability.

• • •

**Across all chronic conditions, the spend adds up to more than $1 trillion.**

• • •

Again, chronic conditions account for 90% of all healthcare costs. This bears repeating because it demands a complete change in perspective on how we are addressing this problem. The structural architecture that exists today is outdated, exposing four key points of impact:

1. Moral consideration: When a system is so clearly failing so

[14] Hamel, Liz, et al. "The Burden of Medical Debt: Results from the Kaiser Family Foundation/New York Times Medical Bills Survey." *The Henry J. Kaiser Family Foundation*, 12 Apr. 2016, www.kff.org/health-costs/report/the-burden-of-medical-debt-results-from-the-kaiser-family-foundationnew-york-times-medical-bills-survey/view/print/.

[15] Montagne, Christina. "NerdWallet Health Finds Medical Bankruptcy Accounts for Majority of Personal Bankruptcies." *NerdWallet*, 7 Aug. 2017, www.nerdwallet.com/blog/health/medical-bankruptcy/?trk_location=ssrp&trk_query=medical%2Bbills%2Bbankruptcy&trk_page=1&trk_position=7.

[16] "Economic Costs of Diabetes in the U.S. in 2017." Diabetes Care, American Diabetes Association, 1 May 2018, care.diabetesjournals.org/content/41/5/917.

[17] Benjamin EJ, et al. "Heart Disease And Stroke Statistics—2017 Updates." 2017;135(10):e146–e603.

[18] "National Diabetes Statistics Report, 2017." Atlanta, GA: *Centers for Disease Control and Prevention*, U.S. Dept of Health and Human Services;

[19] (Benjamin et al.)

24

many of its participants, isn't there a societal obligation to address these issues? And if so, what sector of society is best empowered to come up with the solutions?

2. Economic stability: When so many people are bearing such excessive costs, doesn't that create an undue burden on both individual and societal budgets?

3. Possible trade-offs: These costs not only pull resources from other places they're needed, but also create pressure on an already overwhelmed healthcare system, making everything function less efficiently.

4. Business opportunities: Finally, this is where we need to challenge our entrepreneurial energy to launch solutions to these problems.

When I first met Livongo's founder, Glen Tullman, I asked, "So, you're building a company to manage a condition that I really hope goes away. Do you want the company to win, or do you want a cure for diabetes?"

"Yes, I absolutely want a cure," Glen answered, "but that's going to take some time. And in the meantime, we have to keep people healthy until we do. If there is a way to build a company that helps improve the lives of people with diabetes, then that seems worth doing."

Like me, Glen has a lot at stake in this business of improving the lives of people with chronic conditions. His son, Sam, was diagnosed with type 1 diabetes at the age of eight. Glen shares the story, and still gets emotional, about that first hospital visit, when Sam looked at him and asked, "Dad, can you fix this?" He must have felt exactly like my own dad that day, and he said, without knowing how, that he would. His life changed that day, but it wasn't until years later that Glen was presented with the opportunity to get involved in a much bigger way than he ever imagined.

Glen was on the board of the Juvenile Diabetes Research Foundation, raising money for a cure, running galas and walks, and doing everything he could do. Then an entrepreneur walked through the door with one of the first cellular-enabled blood glucose meters ever invented, knowing he needed money and experienced leaders to refine and scale his invention. He wasn't the right person, but Glen was. And so, with some cajoling from his longtime business partner, Lee Shapiro, Glen put the technology to work in a real way, later adding partner Hemant Taneja, of General Catalyst, to found Livongo. Glen jumped in as CEO, the first salesperson, and doer of everything else that needed to be done.

The initial idea was to sell to large health systems, a group Glen and Lee knew well from their days at Allscripts, which was, at the time, the leading electronic prescribing, practice management, and electronic health record company for physician practices. And it wasn't long before they put together their core crew: Joe Carey, Chief Operating Officer; Amar Kendale, SVP of business development; and Jim Pursley, Chief Commercial Officer.

Livongo's mission appealed to me, of course. But I was excited, too, because I saw clearly what we could create together and what I could add to their story – more data science, a focus on treating the whole person, and an intense clinical rigor to driving and measuring outcomes. Meeting with the early team, I sensed a unique kind of momentum that was very different from what I had seen in other newly minted Silicon Valley healthcare startups, which began with great promise and then failed when they couldn't provide all the clinical improvements and cost savings they promised. This team was different.

Here the idea was to combine the consumer savvy and tech expertise of Silicon Valley with the deep understanding of healthcare. Our team is fundamentally aligned around core concepts that we believe, once embraced, will turbocharge the rate of change in medical care today. We started with some of these at the outset; others we learned how to implement along the way (sometimes clumsily, occasionally gracefully). These concepts are hybrids, syntheses, and evolutions of various innovations that have already driven explosive – even legendary – growth for some of the most successful companies in Silicon Valley, whether it's AirBnB, Netflix, or Slack.

So what happens when you apply similar principles to empowering people with chronic conditions? We know we have only begun to scratch the surface, but even this early, the results of our work have been impressive. We are making people's lives better, creating an experience our members love, and improving their overall health. We are proud of our net promoter score (NPS) of +64.[20]

• • •

**The idea was to combine the consumer savvy and tech expertise of Silicon Valley with the deep understanding of healthcare.**

• • •

Measuring HbA1c is an important indicator of how well blood glucose has been managed over a three-month period. One study revealed Livongo members had achieved the goal set by the American Diabetes Association, a reduction in mean HbA1c from 7.8 % to 6.9%, and maintain this out for three years. A substantial measured improvement like that could reduce the likelihood of long-term complications such as kidney failure, blindness, heart attacks, and strokes.[21]

Further, we have shown that Livongo delivers savings to our clients of more than $100 per member, per month. If you think about the size of our Fortune 500 clients – and the prevalence of diabetes in the

20. https://www.livongo.com/impact.html
21. Ray, Kausik K et al. "Effect Of Intensive Control Of Glucose On Cardiovascular Outcomes And Death In Patients With Diabetes Mellitus: A Meta-Analysis Of Randomised Controlled Trials". The Lancet, vol 373, no. 9677, 2009, pp. 1765-1772. Elsevier BV, doi:10.1016/s0140-6736(09)60697-8.

workforce today – the numbers quickly add up to many millions of dollars already saved by our clients with our program. A case study at Jefferson Health illustrates these outcomes:

- Net Promoter Score of +67
- 1.4-point reduction in HbA1c
- 23% reduction in medical costs with a resulting 3.2x ROI
- 39% reduction of in-patient visits
- 28% reduction in ER visits

Jefferson Health CEO Dr. Stephen Klasko puts it this way:

> It is important that we begin to use technology to finally have healthcare join the consumer revolution. We need to move from hospitals to healthcare with no address.

What are the insights and tools that make this kind of impact possible? I'd like to begin by listing the core ideas driving Livongo today, first by explaining a bit about them and what they mean outside the boundaries of our business, then diving into how they are making a difference for us. My hope is that this provides a roadmap to your own business adventure, the next important world-changing company, or across any other field a curious and motivated mind might want to take it.

# JEFFERSON HEALTH NORTHEAST RESULTS OVER ONE YEAR

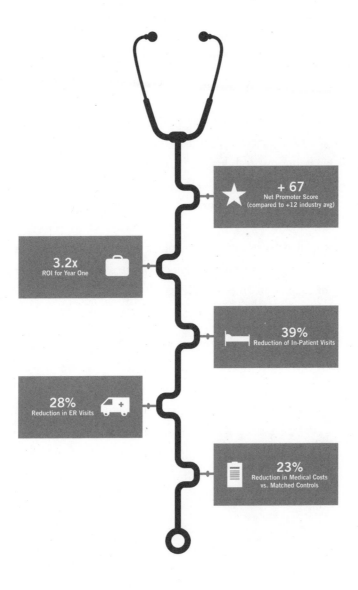

## *Chapter Two Summary: Creating the Map*

- The cost of treating chronic conditions is an increasing and unsustainable burden on the U.S. population and economy.

- The crises created by the impact of chronic conditions provide four key points of impact:
  - Moral consideration,
  - Economic stability,
  - The possible trade-offs, and
  - Business opportunities.

- Livongo drives valuable outcomes: an experience members love. Measurable, sustainable effects on member health. Improved financial outcomes for clients.

30

# CHAPTER 3

# *The Empowered Consumer*

IT WAS ONLY A FEW HUNDRED YEARS ago that knowledge was completely centralized. Literacy was limited and confined to cathedrals, palaces, and universities. The aristocracy controlled the creation and spread of knowledge. It wasn't the best system, but it was all we had. The first revolution was the printing press. Because of that invention, knowledge – and the power that came with it – was decentralized.

It was the same with medicine, and doctors built their own cathedrals, called hospitals. Next to the church, these were generally the largest buildings in any community. If you wanted help, you had to find your way there. Doctors were revered, and people waited in line to see them. Over centuries, there were some slight investments to improve the experience of the people seeking doctors. But these improvements really made it only as far as having a coffee maker in the corner and some magazines in the waiting room.

Then, of course, the internet happened, challenging every one of civilization's centralized systems of information – from travel agents

31

(who controlled access to plane tickets) to mapmakers to printers of encyclopedias. Tools arose that gave the consumer more control of how they worked, shopped, relaxed, traveled, and managed their lives. This was the era of "empowering" the consumer. Sitting in Peoria, Memphis, or Marin, consumers could now browse Harrod's in London, search vacation spots on Expedia, or get an MBA from Chapel Hill. Walls came down, doors opened, and the world would never be the same again.

When the Affordable Care Act (ACA) came along, we began to see shifts in the healthcare market. The ACA shined a bright light on the numbers of – and costs for – uninsured people and brought "pre-existing conditions" into the lexicon of every family and politician in the country. It also brought the consumer face-to-face with the health plan industry. All of a sudden an economy built on selling from a business to another business and then to a consumer (B2B2C) had to also find a way to support a business selling directly to a consumer (D2C), and it had a year to do it. Almost overnight you started to hear health plans refer to themselves as "Health Services" companies. Multimillion-dollar consumer experience and design projects were launched across America's largest health plans as they tried to change and deliver an experience focused on the individual. Some healthcare companies, like Cambia Health Solutions – a total health solutions company that includes health plans within its portfolio – made successful strides in this direction under the leadership of Mark Ganz. "We're reimagining and reshaping the healthcare system to one that is accountable to individuals and families," says Ganz. The landscape had changed, and now the individual mattered more.

Almost inevitably, we arrived at this point where the consumer, who had become incredibly empowered in every other aspect of their life – education, travel, material goods – was looking for (actually, expecting) a similar experience in healthcare. In his book, *On Our Terms: Empowering the New Health Consumer*, Glen Tullman wrote:

> The emergence of this new kind of health consumer has led to a watershed moment that will increasingly call into question why the system cannot provide the same information and service experience as today's most forward-thinking and innovative enterprises – such as Amazon and Uber – who combine digital smarts with services in ways that increase satisfaction, demand, and a willingness to pay![1]

In other words, today, people – as empowered consumers – have a very different attitude when it comes to addressing their medical needs. They'll no longer say, "Okay, I get it. I'll come exactly when you want. I'll interrupt my day. I'll leave work." Instead, this new kind of health consumer says, "Why is this experience bad? Why must I wait for hours and pay so much?"

Think about how DoorDash, the food-delivery service, attacks the three Cs, confusion, complexity, and cost. You used to order from a coffee-stained menu that was piled up behind the phone, calling the restaurant directly, often wondering if the person on the other end of the phone even understood you. Then you wondered where the delivery person was. Then you worried about how much you should tip. Not to mention that fun, last-minute panic of "Wait, do I have cash?" With DoorDash, you order and pay on its app, which keeps you updated as to how close your food is, and the tip is included. Think about all the confusion and complexity that have been eliminated. There is some extra cost, but it's mitigated by the ease of payment, and honestly, in the end you have satisfied customers, because they

[1] Tullman, Glen E et al. On Our Terms: Empowering The New Health Consumer. Magnusson-Skor Publishing, Inc., 2018.

are at the center of the equation. People will pay when the cost equals time saved plus convenience.

People living with chronic conditions are looking for the healthcare version of DoorDash. Now that they know what empowered service is, they no longer accept passively sitting on the sidelines and abiding by the rules of healthcare's legacy systems. Rather, they are looking for something new that puts them in control, just as they are when they make a restaurant reservation with OpenTable or plan a trip on Expedia. With smartphone in hand, they can seek and find the products and services that fit them best. They are no longer isolated and alone on this journey. They can easily get opinions about a brand based on the real experiences of people like them – and people are more than willing to share their stories and opinions.

**• • •**
**They are looking for something new that puts them in control, just as they are when they make a restaurant reservation.**
**• • •**

All of this is the result of an enormous shift in the focus on our systems. Twenty-five years ago, they were fundamentally focused on logistics, centralization, and efficiency. The customer's needs came somewhere near the end of that hierarchy, mostly because it was so difficult to accomplish anything. In order to make any system work, you needed to bundle it together into a conglomerate stack, which was not the most elegant system for getting the customer what they needed. Hemant Taneja eloquently explained how all this changed in his book, *Unscaled: How AI and a New Generation of Upstarts Are Creating the Economy of the Future.*

Throughout the twentieth century, technology and economics drove a dominant logic: bigger was almost always better.

34

Around the world the goal was to build bigger corporations, bigger hospitals, bigger governments, bigger schools and banks and farms and electric grids and media conglomerates. It was smart to scale up – to take advantage of classic economies of scale.

In the twenty-first century, technology and economics are driving the opposite – an unscaling of business and society. This is far more profound than just startups disrupting established firms. The dynamic is in the process of unraveling all the previous century's scale into hyper-focused markets. Artificial intelligence (AI) and a wave of AI-propelled technologies are allowing innovators to effectively compete against economies of scale with what I call the economies of unscale. This huge shift is remaking massive, deeply rooted industries such as energy, transportation, and healthcare, opening up fantastic possibilities for entrepreneurs, imaginative companies, and resourceful individuals.[2]

Additionally, digital transformation has also allowed companies to create dialogues with their customers – either actual or with invisible digital information – to help better understand their wants and needs. Empowered consumers can raise their voices. Smart companies listen and respond. At every step along the way, data is collected.

If this feels somewhat obvious, it's because we're all swept up in it. We participate in every aspect of our lives and see it driving every other industry forward. The reason it's worth noting here is because the medical industry has failed to embrace this change. Twenty-five years after the launch of Netscape and more than a decade after Steve Jobs

---

[2] Taneja, Hemant, and Kevin Maney. Unscaled: How A.I. And A New Generation Of Upstarts Are Creating The Economy Of The Future. Piatkus, 2018.

gave us the iPhone, it is stunning how little our healthcare industry has adapted to the potential impact of these profoundly remarkable tools.

## *Chapter Three Summary: The Empowered Consumer*

- The world has changed dramatically for the consumer, but not for the consumer as "patient" when it comes to healthcare, which was built on the model of economies of scale – the idea that bigger is better.

- The internet empowered consumers, and tools arose that gave the consumer more control of how they worked, shopped, relaxed, traveled, and managed their lives.

- Now that consumers know what empowered service is, they will no longer accept passively sitting on the sidelines and abiding by the rules of healthcare's legacy systems. Patients are not patient anymore.

- "Artificial intelligence (AI) and a wave of AI-propelled technologies are allowing innovators to effectively compete against economies of scale" – a concept that Hemant Taneja refers to as the economies of unscale – opening up exciting possibilities.

- Digital transformation has also allowed companies to create dialogues with their customers to help better understand their wants and needs. Empowered consumers can raise their voices. Smart companies listen and respond.

- Up to this point, the medical industry has largely failed to embrace this dynamic.

# CHAPTER **4**

# *The Power of Love*

THERE WAS A TIME when service economy workers were all somewhere on a spectrum between diner waitress and brain surgeon. In other words, you were either at the beck and call of your customer ("Tell the chef I want the Denver omelet but with Swiss cheese and pineapple") or you were totally in control (um, nobody tells a brain surgeon how to do their job). In our new world, there are a lot more waitresses than brain surgeons, as the empowered consumer is now calling more and more of the shots. It's like when you're driving along listening to your Google Maps directions and you don't go the way she wants you to go. You can almost hear the robot grit her teeth as she says, "One moment, rerouting…" But within seconds she gives you another route, because you are the one in control.

In such a world, the service industry needs to carefully choose where it stands. On one end of this spectrum, there's Walmart, the largest employer in America. It has 90% of the population living

---

[1] Ladd, Brittain. "Playing To Its Strengths: Why Walmart Must Focus On Its Stores And Logistics.", *Forbes Magazine*, 10 Sept. 2018, www.forbes.com/sites/brittainladd/2018/09/09/playing-to-its-strengths-why-walmart-must-focus-on-groceries-stores-and-logistics/#396e26081e06.

within ten miles of one of its stores.[1] Its key mission is to provide low-cost products to its customers and, to date, that focus has served the company well. For a long time, because of its size and scale, there was no competition that could hold a candle to Walmart.

But today, things have changed. The company is feeling the pressure, as Amazon – with its automated fulfillment, AI-powered logistics, and e-commerce as well as innovations in their digital assistant, Echo (aka Alexa), AI-powered AWS (Amazon Web Services), and Amazon Go – takes center stage in the customer-centric world. Now Walmart is being forced to invest and innovate. It is also beginning to think about its customer in a way it hasn't before. Because suddenly, in a world of same-day delivery, being a mere five miles away is like being on the other side of the world.

A decade ago, the marketer Kevin Roberts came out with the concept of Lovemarks. This was the idea that brands were becoming passé and that Lovemarks were companies that consumers would pay a premium for because of their loyalty and affection. These days, it's not about paying a premium, it's about not paying anything at all. When Uber was getting headlines for being a less-than-admirable company, thousands of people shifted over to Lyft. It wasn't difficult. It literally was as simple as clicking one button less than an inch away from the other. People used to love Facebook, but those feelings have grown complicated, and consequently, there is probably an opportunity in the market for some other social network.

It's not hard to figure out why the healthcare industry isn't loved. It's composed of companies that were started, merged, migrated, went public, got acquired, consolidated, and rebranded. Walking through many urban hospitals can feel as if you're inside a battleship that has been patched up and sent out from the docks barely seaworthy. These institutions have been working for decades to cut costs and create efficiencies, but often doing so with little thought of adding value to the customer. The scars show.

We know that love is a key ingredient to our story. Not like. Love. Being liked is waiting to be gone. You have to be loved for staying power. We need our members to keep loving the experience we bring, so that they continue participating, which will improve their health and drive savings for our clients. Which is why we're as obsessed with keeping our net promoter score as high as Netflix's. People do not care how much you know until they know how much you care.

Think about what it means to be a Software as a Service (SaaS) company in this day and age: Shopify is an amazing service for shop owners, but if Stripe comes up with a more intuitive and easier way to bundle social, web, inventory, checkout, and connect with your accountant, well, there's no reason that any retailer is going to stay with Shopify. Same with OpenTable or even a giant like Ticketmaster. It seems like every time you turn around there's a new, more convenient, more intuitive, less expensive service being offered. Everyone liked AOL, MySpace, and Yahoo, until they didn't.

- - -

**Being liked is waiting to be gone. You have to be loved for staying power.**

- - -

## Building Tools That People Love

So, we knew that the customer was ready. This really was our key insight at Livongo, that once consumers experienced empowerment in one aspect of their lives, they would expect it in every other part, especially the most important parts. Not merely in the healthcare system, but everywhere their health was affected, at home, on the go, any place interaction was possible. After all, if Delta can inform you that your bag is on the plane, surely we could manage to alert a member that their glucose was low. If TaskRabbit can drop off your dry cleaning, then Livongo should be able to deliver glucose strips to your doorstep. If Strava can track your morning run, certainly Livongo could keep track of your prescriptions. By utilizing technology that has already been embraced everywhere else in their life, we knew we could serve people better.

We started with a cellular-connected, two-way messaging blood glucose meter. So, whenever a member checked their blood glucose, we would instantaneously respond with a personalized direct message to them. For people with diabetes, capturing blood glucose values often is a pain, requiring them to write it in a logbook or continuously establish a Bluetooth connection. So we eliminated that. No Bluetooth connections, no asking people to do extra steps to record and write down their results. We empowered people by having them do less and get more value. In addition, every time they interacted with us, they received more personalized and actionable digital coaching touch points. For example, if someone with type 2 diabetes had a blood glucose of 220 mg/dL after lunch,* we might encourage them to drink a glass of water, walk for fifteen minutes, and recheck their blood glucose. And because we knew how many checks they were doing, we could automatically send a refill of strips directly to their door. The whole experience is seamless and easy, they are getting more without doing more, and we are learning more with every interaction, so that every experience is more personalized and valuable.

We also built systems where members could connect to a larger community, further connecting neighbors, colleagues, and the people they love. It's the members' choice – they can share their readings with whomever they choose, conveniently and easily. For example,

---

*Up to 180 mg/dL is normal two hours after eating.

someone might decide to have their wife notified via text when they were less than 54 mg/dL, but then and only then. So even though we can't be there to get a glass of juice for our members when their blood glucose is low, we can reach out to the people around them, serving as a powerful link in their support network. And Livongo is available twenty-four hours a day, seven days a week, 365 days a year. Because when you live with a chronic condition, you never get a break. Not one single day off. So we do not take one either.

We also let people directly schedule coaching sessions when it works for them. This connects them with someone who is incredibly well-trained, has access to their medical info, and whose only purpose is to empower them. The member isn't charged by the call. It's there whenever they need it. This was the promise we brought to life – a system built with empowered consumers in the center, providing them deep personalization and allowing them to receive the experience they wanted, when they wanted it. As one of our members put it, talking about their Certified Diabetes Educator (CDE):

41

> If I need to talk to a CDE or want to ask, "Hey, can you kind of refresh my memory what food to stay away from?" I can send an email, I can schedule a coaching session. I get time to talk to a CDE and it's included. Like, really? It's included. I just have to find the time slot that's open on their calendar. That's it. I'm like, "Wow. I'm not actually paying for this conversation." This is mind-blowing. This is included in my membership. This is huge for me.

Once we had converted that technology to serve the needs of people with chronic conditions, we were able to start connecting and building their trust, from their experiences in ways that helped us to serve not just them individually, but ultimately the entire community. We now had the ability to build a new system that was both sustainable and scalable across populations. We were on our way, building a seamless system that mirrors current consumer expectations, providing members ease in finding products, services, and advice that suited them best.

The last hurdle was that we had to make something that wasn't just functional. It needed to do more than just "work." There had to be an emotional halo so bright that members wouldn't simply like us, they would love us. Because in the new empowered landscape, a brand is either loved, or it's gone.

### *Chapter Four Summary: The Power of Love*

- The new consumer-centric world is forcing the service industry to reevaluate the way it does business.

- Surfacing during the past decade was the concept of Lovemarks, the idea that brand loyalty had shifted from one of respect based on intellect to one based on love, an emotional response building loyalty that "goes beyond reason."

- The healthcare industry is not loved, and it's easy to see why: The institutions have focused on cutting costs and creating efficiencies, with little thought about value-add for the customer.

- The environment created an opportunity for a customer-centric company like Livongo.

- Customers love the experience we create, and our aim is to keep our NPS right up there with that of Netflix.

# CHAPTER 5

# *Empathy First*

IN ORDER TO BUILD a customer-centric product that people will emotionally connect with, you have to start with empathy. First, plot out what your audience's problems are, developing what the late, great Tom Main of Oliver Wyman termed a "hassle map" of key pain points on their journey. Once any company identifies the pain points, it can then design from there. Our research on this, predictably, uncovered a wealth of pain, a lot of noise, and a ton of opportunity.

Almost anyone can at least partially relate to some of the pain points or parts of the current healthcare system that need fixing: waiting in line, difficulty getting a timely appointment, taking time out of a workday then being made to wait for hours, getting a needle stuck in a vein for lab work that gets lost, and of course, the endless bills that come for months. The vast majority of us have lived through it, in some manner. For many who have a medical crisis – a planned surgery, a pregnancy, or limited treatment – navigating the healthcare system, while confusing and irksome, is a short-lived episode where

43

the positives ultimately far outweigh the negatives. But for someone with a chronic condition, all that noise can be incredibly discouraging, debilitating, and ultimately harmful.

The noise in the healthcare system – confusion, complexity, and cost – creates an unbearable amount of commotion. The most empathetic thing we could do was silence that noise. Clearly, we're not the only sector to suffer from the issue, and it's interesting to examine how other industries have been transformed.

One of the earliest sectors to change was also one of the noisiest: the financial-services market. Long before ETrade and other financial dot-coms challenged the system, even before the ATM made cash easily accessible, Charles Schwab built an empire around creating an all-new approach, a customer-oriented financial-services business. Schwab made it radically simple, building an entire system that methodically removed all the pain points for people wanting to invest in the market. It made its entire system one where, instead of brokers offering advice, it just took the orders from the customer, exponentially reducing the confusion. It changed from a commission-based system to a salary-based system, reducing the complexity. Most importantly, it cut fees, reducing the costs. By creating a company that reduced the three Cs for its customer, Schwab was able to ignite the consumer-based financial revolution that thrives today.

Think about how far that system has evolved. For large purchases – buying a house, financing a car – there is still complexity.

> **• • •**
> **The noise in the healthcare system – confusion, complexity, and cost creates an unbearable amount of commotion. The most empathetic thing we could do was silence that noise.**
> **• • •**

Those transactions are equivalent to the kind of acute care that the medical industry manages extremely well: getting a hip replaced, or having a baby. But for the smaller, everyday financial transactions – the stuff more analogous to managing chronic conditions – we're living in a very different world. You're depositing checks to Citi from your phone, rounding up extra savings on Acorn, and paying your babysitter via Venmo. Imagine if we had that kind of convenience in healthcare.

One difference, though, is that the financial-services industry actually deliberately wanted to be noisy and intimidating. It had no empathy for its customers and knew perfectly well how terrible it was for them, but until Chuck Schwab showed up, the industry was pretty happy to keep it that way. After all, that's how it justified all its high fees.

In contrast, for most of the players in our system, the health-services industry actually doesn't want to be as loud as it is, it just can't help itself. The doctors in the system are generally working to abide by the Hippocratic Oath, the modern version of which says that doctors' responsibilities include understanding how illnesses "may affect the person's family and economic stability."[1] But the industry is a mess born from the frictional marriage of multiple, competing systems. The confusion, complexity, and cost are being constantly amplified by the healthcare industry – by both the establishment and new entrants – which has created an overwhelming cacophony for consumers, and a serious detriment for those of us living with chronic conditions.

Our hassle map discovered quite a few addressable items. Once we found them, we were able to develop a response that removed the hassle and quieted the noise. Here are a few of those hassles:

---

[1] Lasagna, Louis. "A Modern Hippocratic Oath." Various Physicians Oaths, Association of American Physicians and Surgeons, www.aapsonline.org/ethics/oaths.htm#lasagna.

*Hassle #1:* I know I need to check my blood glucose levels, but strips are expensive. Moreover, if I check as frequently as my doctor suggests, I run out of strips toward the end of the month.

*Solution:* Free strips.

*Hassle #2:* I often forget to bring my blood glucose meter to my appointment. Or I forget my logbook of blood glucose readings at home. Or I change meters and my doctor doesn't have the dongle to download my information.

*Solution:* Provide a cellular blood glucose meter to capture the data in a way that makes it super easy to share with doctors and anyone else in the system.

*Hassle #3:* I cannot always remember what my numbers should be when I am checking, or what to do about them.

*Solution:* Create personalized responses sent to members through the blood glucose meter.

Those are just some of the pain points we have been able to effectively address. But it is easy to see how even just these three interlink to create a more complete ecosystem. With this approach we were able to eliminate hassles in a more holistic, supportive, and cost-effective way.

## Chapter Five Summary: Empathy First

- To build empathy, we developed a "hassle map" of key pain points in people's journeys. Our hassle map uncovered myriad addressable pain points and, consequently, a ton of opportunity.

- Confusion, complexity, and cost have existed in other systems, like the financial market, where innovators have reduced all three. The healthcare market can do the same.

- By building a complete ecosystem, you can eliminate multiple pain points more effectively.

47

# CHAPTER 6

## *Technology Is Only As Great As the Experience It Helps to Deliver*

AT LIVONGO, WE TRULY believe that words matter. As Glen Tullman is fond of saying "If you want to change the world, you have to change the words." The language we use to describe issues holds enormous sway over the way we feel and think about them. While linguistics may not define our reality, it undeniably has enormous influence over our perceptions, and one of the surest ways to create substantive change in the way we see things is to refine the way we say them.

So we start with this one absurdly simple premise: None of our members ever wanted to have a chronic condition. After the scary swerve of their first diagnosis, every single member found themselves on a new road, an off-ramp onto a journey not one of them wanted to take. Furthermore, because each person is so much more than just a member, we must understand and embrace their unique and very personal challenges in order to properly treat them as a human being, not a condition and not a number.

And we begin with words.

When someone is diagnosed with diabetes, they are not suddenly transformed into the sum total of their condition; they are still a person first – a person living with a chronic condition. Instead of being a "diabetic," they are a person living with diabetes. I'm amazed that the word "diabetic" still persists at all, frankly, considering that also in the Hippocratic Oath (just before the part about appreciating the patient's life circumstances) it says, "I will remember that I do not treat a fever chart, a cancerous growth, but a sick human being."[1] In other words, the condition is not the person.

Similarly, when someone wants to know where their blood glucose level is at a current moment, they do not "test," because that implies that they will either pass or fail. Rather, they "check." It's a small tweak in terminology, but one that shows an understanding of how people can often feel interrogated or judged. A great example of this is when people joke with me about the answers they give their doctor when they're asked how much they drink. "I knock the number in half," a friend said.

• • •

**We do not "help" our members. Instead, we empower them. We prompt, we support, we encourage.**

• • •

The truth is, people are nervous, afraid of being judged. We need to acknowledge this truth if we truly want to provide useful solutions and empower people to use them.

Working in the medical profession, it is very common to hear phrases like "diabetic noncompliance," or "so-and-so had poor control and it led to a diabetic foot complication." It is a judgmental categorization without any recognition of what it is like to live in that world: a place where one must avoid high concentrations of carbohydrates, cakes, pies, and eggnog during the holidays; a life where when you

---

[1] (Lasagna)

do decide to treat yourself, you are chastised for not knowing exactly how to handle the exception – ironically, *because you have so little practice handling it, because you have done such a good job of "avoiding" it in the first place.* (Can you feel my personal frustration here?) At Livongo, we know from experience the challenges, which is why we work hard to recognize and respect how difficult it is. Consequently, we never judge our members. We do not "help" our members. Instead, we empower them. We prompt, we support, we encourage. Every word matters, because words subtly but meaningfully inform not only the way we think, but how we behave.

Respect has a lot of dimensions: sincerity, empathy, and careful listening. Livongo employs a number of trained health professionals we call "coaches." This team interacts with our members when the members need a human touch. Our coaches aren't reading from scripts supplying them with canned responses. For them, it's personal. They aren't responding to hypotheticals or theoreticals, but are engaging with the member's real life and real challenges. One of our coaches, Holly Lemmons, summed up working with a struggling member this way:

> We have several planned sessions with the members, so we can get a pretty good idea of what's working and what's not. If a member set a goal to grocery shop and cook more often, and he tells me that his workload increased and he has to depend on fast food, I might say, "Okay, this whole cooking healthy food isn't working for you right now, so let's figure out how you can eat out and make better choices." If he says he goes to McDonald's, KFC, and Taco Bell, I can send him information about the items on each menu that he can choose in order to stay in control. Again, we have to meet members where they are.

Or, as another coach, Morgan Robbins, put it, "I'm in my members' pocket 24/7. They can text me and say, 'Hey, Morgan, I'm in a restaurant. What would you recommend on this menu?' and send me a picture."

Tailoring our suggestions in this way is critical. Members who are truck drivers, for example, are often dependent on drive-through restaurants because they can't stop. For them, we can customize recommendations so that they're not just the healthiest but also the most hand-friendly. It's only by listening carefully that we gain the insights that, in turn, lead to these sorts of meaningful and empowering suggestions.

## Going Further

Think about all the hassles and obstacles someone with diabetes 51 has to live with. First, you need to constantly be ordering the strips you use to measure your blood glucose levels. Then there is the hassle of negotiating with insurance companies that might have denied strip coverage (this happens at times because, despite your doctor asking you to check your blood glucose level five to seven times per day, your insurance company might cover only enough for three times a day.) Then there is recording and tracking the values, figuring out the monitoring equipment, not to mention managing copays, appointments, etc. Anyone looking at it can clearly see that it completely sucks.

We ran across an interesting company designed to address type 1 diabetes called MySugr, whose slogan was "Make Diabetes Suck Less." I had a lot of respect for the frank way it addressed the issue with that line. There was an empathy in the recognition that the day-to-day treatment of diabetes is just a big drag. That shouldn't be a radical insight, but in the world of healthcare, it actually is. The industry has a horrible tendency to get in its own way and not see the person, the patient, whoever is going through the process. Unfortunately for MySugr, it only made things slightly better, not different. In the end, it just wasn't comprehensive enough to eradicate all those pain points and make it suck a lot less. Sometimes it's not about adapting to or trying to improve a failing system, it's about coming up with a better one. You have to reduce everything to the foundation and rebuild. Or, just come up with something completely new.

Once we understood that, creating an experience that was the total opposite of everything the consumer had previously experienced was a relatively straightforward process. Straightforward, but not simple. It was hard work. And our team did an amazing job.

We turned the experience upside down. Unlimited and free strips delivered to your door before you needed them, access to well-trained coaches, twenty-four hours a day, seven days a week; blood pressure and weight readings that are automatically captured through cellular transmission; insights and health nudges with relevant and timely information; monitoring that is smart enough to know when you need encouragement and exactly what sort of encouragement you need.

## *The Connected Experience*

In a well-architected system, you drive better outcomes by being deliberate about the objectives and optimizing for each person in ways you think they can best achieve those goals. In the world of chronic conditions, for example, it's not about simply getting more data to doctors. Providers (and prescribers) are important in this system, but because people with chronic conditions spend 99.9% of their lives outside the hospital (hopefully), the person we design solutions for is going to have relatively little interaction with doctors. The doctor plays the role of educating, diagnosing, and prescribing. But the actual face time during a doctor visit is still a mere twenty minutes,[2] and even people with chronic conditions who are "persistent high users" of medical services see their primary care physician only an average of 5.2 times a year.[3] So the amount of education that can be delivered in that short a time is inherently limited. (Imagine trying to teach a child to read or trying to learn a foreign language with that amount of instruction.) For every problem, finding the solution continually brings us back to building a system that is customer-centric, one that truly understands and supports what customers are experiencing every day and puts them back in charge.

When I say our members need tools that empower them, I don't mean it metaphorically or philosophically – I mean it in a very practical, hands-on way. When we asked an outside design firm to help us develop a new blood glucose meter and carrying case, it integrated a receptacle within the lancing device for used lancets. This feature took up a lot of space in the device because, as the designers explained, one should change the lancet every time a member pricks his finger. These designers had diligently educated themselves on the rules, had read the FDA guidelines, and knew what the best practices were. But we knew that in reality, most people change their lancet only once or twice a month, when it gets dull, or when someone else pricks their finger with it. Designers were coming up with smart and fancy "lancet-disposal products" that most members simply did not use or want. From that moment onward, we knew we had to bring our product design work in-house.

Of course, that's an exceptional example of how our experience and understanding leads us to create products and services focused

---

[2] Ray, Kristin N., et al. "Opportunity Costs of Ambulatory Medical Care in the United States." AJMC, www.ajmc.com/journals/issue/2015/2015-vol21-n8/opportunity-costs-of-ambulatory-medical-care-in-the-united-states?p=1.
[3] Bresnick, Jennifer. "Chronic Disease Management Costs 17 Times More than Average." HealthITAnalytics, 22 Apr. 2015, healthitanalytics.com/news/chronic-disease-management-costs-17-times-more-than-average.

on our members' real-world needs. For people with diabetes, the experience of receiving a blood glucose meter is fairly bland, even disappointing. You usually have to go to the pharmacy and pick out a meter made of cheap plastic surrounded by a flimsy case that is embarrassingly ugly, even for the fashion non-elite. We ship our blood glucose meter to the member and have designed one of the best "unboxing" experiences in the world of diabetes. Similar to the feel when you open an Apple product, the packaging and unboxing experience are intended to deliver delight and communicate instant value. And thoughtful design of the presentation also makes a difference. For example, we learned that ensuring that the battery charger can be easily found triggers fewer member-support questions about battery life. So instead of discreetly tucking it away in the bottom of the box, we put it front and center so that a member would just know, without even having to read the instructions, that this is a rechargeable device. Making everything about every experience easy, simple, and intuitive was how we were going to reduce the noise.

Finally, there is the way our products connect, which combines IQ with a healthy dose of EQ. It may be cheaper to rely on Bluetooth, but we know that every extra step we ask a member to perform increases the complexity and noise in the experience that we want to lower. We had seen competitors like Glooko never quite master a user-friendly model (starting with a cable connection, then migrating to Bluetooth to ensure data-uploading capabilities). Neither worked well, and users hated the extra steps. We needed to be different by being intuitive and easy, even if it added to the cost on our end. For instance, it would have been even less expensive to make the whole system manual, requiring the members to record, log, and journal everything. But that would have lowered reporting accuracy and frequency, increased latency, and ultimately would have been far less helpful in improving their health. Instead, we concentrated on enabling our devices to have their own cellular connection so that data was constantly streaming, without interruption. Choosing tools that acknowledged and anticipated real human behavior increased our short-term costs, but our bet was that by increasing effectiveness, they would drive long-term savings even higher, all while fulfilling our mission of empowering individuals to get better.

Today, Livongo combines smart connected devices and the cloud to empower members to monitor their health (whether it's rising or falling blood pressure or blood glucose, or other issues) and respond to them, if needed. For instance, when a member uses a Livongo blood glucose meter to measure their blood glucose, the information is sent to the cloud. If the reading is above or below their predetermined threshold, they will get a call or a text from a coach within minutes, checking in or offering personalized

• • •

**The three Cs are being disassembled by the potent three Es: empathy, ease, and empowerment.**

• • •

suggestions. The interaction can often save a person from panic or a costly trip to the ER. And importantly, it lets members know that they are never alone. As one of our members who awoke with low blood glucose put it:

> I will tell you, if it weren't for Livongo that day, I don't know what I would have done. I may have gone to the ER and ended up with an enormous, obnoxious copay, but my coach mitigated everything. She kept me calm and told me what to do at a time that was really scary for me.

We also generate reports over time to let people see their blood glucose patterns, which may in turn guide them to make better choices for their health. And, if they are showing improvement, to know that they are on the right track. As another member told us:

> Before, when I was just in denial and I was maybe only checking myself every other day, that one number means nothing, in the scheme of things. But then when you start checking more, and you see the data, and you see how with the disease that number can swing radically, then you realize that one number is just not enough. You can't just do one number every other day, or one number a day. You have to check more consistently. I realize that there is no way that I can manage this disease without this data, and that means I've gotta check. I've just gotta check, every single day, and I've got to take my meds. And once you finally realize all of that, then you just do what you gotta do.

We know – from feedback like this and from data – that what we are doing for our members and for our clients is absolutely working. The combination of our connected devices, prompts, and coaching creates an incredibly effective ecosystem. The three Cs are being disassembled by the potent three Es: empathy, ease, and empowerment.

### Chapter Six Summary: Technology Is Only As Great As the Experience It Helps to Deliver

- We believe that empathy begins with language, so we start with a simple premise: None of our members ever wanted to have a chronic condition. We treat each member as a person, not a disease – our members are not "diabetics."

- We recognize how difficult it is to live with a chronic condition(s), so we never judge our members. We do not "help" our members. Instead, we empower them. We prompt, we support, we encourage.

- Our coaches do not respond to hypotheticals or theoreticals but engage with the member's real life and real challenges. We meet members on their terms.

- We create a customer-centric experience, designing our tools around real human behavior, fulfilling our mission of empowering individuals to get better.

# CHAPTER 7

# *The Slow Revolution*

THERE ARE A NUMBER OF VALID, logical reasons for the slow pace of change in our industry. Part of the problem is the overwhelming scale of the issue. It's a lot easier to disrupt smaller categories. The entire business-travel category, including flights, restaurants, hotels, taxis, etc., is less than 3% of the United States' GDP.[1] Meanwhile, the healthcare industry makes up around 18%,[2] with chronic care making up the lion's share. In *Unscaled*, Taneja provides a concise overview of how this problem achieved such a colossal scale:

> Over the past four or five decades carbohydrate-heavy diets – pushed by mass-market production and mass marketing of cereals and drinks laced with high-fructose corn syrup – created an epidemic of obesity and, ultimately, diabetes. The medical profession lumped most people with diabetes into one of two categories of the disease – type 1 is

---

[1] World Travel & Tourism Council, 2018. United States, https://www.wttc.org/-/media/files/reports/economic-impact-research/countries-2018/unitedstates2018.pdf.

[2] "National Health Expenditures 2017 Highlights." Centers for Medicare and Medicaid Services, 2018, https://www.cms.gov/Research-Statistics-Data-and-Systems/Statistics-Trends-and-Reports/NationalHealthExpendData/Downloads/highlights.pdf.

genetic and type 2 is diet-related — and prescribed a standard treatment. It was a classic mass-market medicine approach. So the healthcare industry scaled up to meet demand. It built diabetes centers and more hospitals and ran every patient, assembly-line style, through the same tests the few times a year they'd be able to visit an endocrinologist, whose schedule was packed. Yet for patients, sugar levels in between appointments can change, rising and falling to dangerous levels, and the disease can progress, adding more costs and more visits to bigger hospitals. People suffering from diabetes end up costing the healthcare system $300 billion a year in the United States alone.[3]

It obviously takes time to turn around an aircraft carrier that big. Additionally, in any large system it's inevitable that there are more than a few vested interests on board who are more concerned with profits than progress and may be slowing that aircraft carrier down.

Clearly, too, we're talking about people's health and well-being, so any system failure could have potentially fatal repercussions. Certainly then, a degree of caution is absolutely prudent and necessary. But there are other cultural causes that drive a sluggish pace of adoption.

The first is how the healthcare field approaches innovation. This industry has an almost intuitive affection for the idea that some new thing will come along and fix the system. Because of this prejudice, we're now an industry that has over-indexed on technology to the nth degree. Empowering the customer in healthcare isn't about a new "thing," it's about a systematic rethinking of the entire approach. In fact, if you look at those tools that have radically changed the life of

3. (Taneja, 2018)

the empowered contemporary consumer – Amazon, Nest, Spotify, etc. – they are fundamentally systems before they are things, systems that *placed the customer firmly at the center*.

The interesting thing about this whole "consumer at the center" idea is that it is the only way innovation on any front can survive. New medications only bring improvements if people take them. The fact is, any silver bullet is useless without a system supporting it that makes it easily accessible for the user, one that encourages and somehow rewards its use.

Another very real factor hindering progress is that this dynamic democratization of information has fundamentally challenged the doctor's historic role in society. Granted, that was already changing. Our collective image of the doctor had already evolved from a genial and unfailing Marcus Welby to a profoundly human Meredith Grey. But our culture has only recently – and only partly – emerged from a place where the M.D. was the community's infallible patriarch, with a status rivaling that of the clergy. There are reasons why we should continue to embrace at least some of that authority – after all, doctors have spent a good chunk of their lives studying how to save our lives – but we should recognize, too, how these authoritative tendencies, when entrenched, often instinctively oppose the innovations that challenge them. Even if doctors were the answer, there are simply not enough of them to treat the 180 million people living with chronic conditions.

Moreover, and probably most important, the healthcare sector can only challenge and change what it can touch, and most of what occurs in chronic care happens outside the walls of any medical industry infrastructure. It's not in a specialist's office, it's not in the OR or ICU. Instead, it's someone staring at an Olive Garden menu wondering what they should order. It's someone sleeping in late instead of getting up and trudging through the snow to a 24 Hour Fitness. In other words, care for chronic conditions is life, 99.99% of which occurs outside the walls of a doctor's office. The industry collectively shrugs when it comes to implementing any sort of revolutionary changes, not because it does not want to help, but because any effective solutions are so beyond its capacity. The system was built for a whole range of completely separate acute conditions.

It comes down to this: If you have an appendix burst in the wilderness, unless they can get you into a hospital and fix what's wrong, you're going to die. So, the system unfailingly endeavors itself to get you to that hospital. That's what it is built to do. But if you have well-managed diabetes in the wilderness, you're going to be able to walk out of there on your own, so, well, enjoy the hike.

The tragedy, of course, is that there is a dichotomy at play. The problem is both urgent and present, creating a dramatic impact on the entire system, clogging the hospitals with costs, eating up medical professionals' hours, and taking attention away from people who could actually use that hands-on care – while at the same time, the problem is abstract and distant, happening very slowly, incrementally, and for the most part, somewhere else. The only solution that would work is one where you met the person where they were, outside the system, and became a part of their everyday lives.

## *Chapter Seven Summary: The Slow Revolution*

- There are valid, logical, and cultural reasons for the slow pace of change in healthcare.

- The healthcare industry is a behemoth, making up almost 20% of the United States' GDP, with chronic care accounting for the lion's share.

- A degree of caution is necessary. A system failure could have fatal repercussions.

- The healthcare industry has an almost intuitive affection for the idea that some new thing will come along and fix the system.

- Our collective image of the doctor has historically been one of the infallible patriarch, and authoritative tendencies often oppose the innovations that challenge them.

- The healthcare sector can only challenge and change what it can touch, and most of what occurs in chronic care happens outside the walls of any medical industry infrastructure.

# Health Versus Healthcare

*HEALTHCARE* IS THE SYSTEM TODAY. It's what the system does (through a variety of medical interventions) to help the patient get better. *Health* is what each person aspires for themselves. Though it involves *wellness* (e.g., diet and exercise), health is also about taking medicine, tracking symptoms, and – if need be – connecting back into the healthcare system.

63

Someone with a chronic condition is caught living in a universe somewhere between these two worlds. That person's needs are greater than what a wellness regimen would cover, because they need to connect back into the healthcare system with greater regularity. Which is why, consequently, patients with chronic conditions are paying the vast majority of the costs that support the healthcare system, a system that is not built specifically for them.

To complicate things even more, everyone within the healthcare system is torn by competing priorities. Care is not the sole mission of the healthcare system. Anytime you enter the healthcare system, you're stepping into a universe where doctors, insurance systems, medical device companies, and the pharmaceutical industry have multiple commitments: seeing lots of patients for short amounts of time, providing cost-effective care, generating profit, and, yes, making the patient better in that moment, but clearly that is not always the first priority. It's a machine. And that machine is making a lot of noise.

Another significant issue that healthcare has today, at least from a consumer perspective, is fiscal accountability. In any other part of the economy, the consumer measures quality against cost. But when you enter the current medical system, it is all completely opaque. As a patient, you probably know what your copay is – though even that might be a surprise once you hit the cashier's window – but you probably have no idea what your insurer or your employer is paying. You also don't know how those costs compare with those of any other hospital, practice, or doctor. There are new regulations forcing hospitals to make their pricing more available and transparent, but efforts to date point to a similarly confusing structure, as the "chargemaster" is not the real price for most people.

Finally, there's no visible correlation between quality and costs. You could be getting excellent care at a reasonable discount or, alternately, paying a premium for someone who is subpar. Today, the ratio of quality to cost is virtually impossible to measure. Right now, people are making choices that have an enormous impact on their personal budgets and their employers' bottom line – oftentimes rewarding organizations that are low quality – because we don't have good information. To overcome this, we must create a standard system that measures quality and makes that information available and understandable. Only then will the consumer be properly empowered to make smarter, better decisions.

## A Better System

What would an ideal system for people with chronic conditions actually look like? A decade ago, I took a class from a leading health economist titled "Fee-for-Service Is Dead," the argument being that the world was moving toward a model where doctors and hospitals only got paid or reimbursed when things actually worked. But here we are, all these years later, and this prediction remains largely unrealized. The fee-for-service model is alive and well and entrenched in systems that make billions from it. So if we want to create something more effective, we'll have to create a system where we get rewarded for positive outcomes, not simply for doing the work.

So, stepping back and looking at it all objectively, the question is, if we were to invent a system from scratch to deliver care for the person with a chronic condition, what are the principles that we would put into place and design for?

- Put the person with the chronic condition at the center, and design around their needs. This means the supporting staff, providers, and shareholders are important but secondary.

- Make it always available, 24/7/365, because people with chronic conditions never get a day off. In fact, they never even get a minute off.

- Get paid only when things work, when the member is using the service and benefiting from it. (Your local gym uses the inverse of this model, making money by you not coming, which may partly explain why so many Americans are overweight.) To create real change, then, payment should go only to systems,

65

services, and medications that are effective.

- Allocate existing resources with the people who will benefit the most. Today, everyone is seen by a provider, which means less access for the people who are actually in more need. People with chronic conditions are filling up an overburdened and expensive system that isn't designed to manage their needs efficiently. If we could effectively prioritize those needs, every element of the system – whether it was the medical professional or medication – would be able to practice at the top of its license. To make this work, we would have to design a system where fewer people were seeing a doctor or visiting an office to get counsel and care. It sounds counterintuitive, unless, of course, they got healthier and happier somewhere outside the system. Providing tools for people to manage their condition outside the system would free up doctors, giving them the bandwidth to care for the 20% of the people who drive 80% of the costs.[1] It would also give them time to serve the under-resourced people, who eventually end up unhealthy, unhappy, and costing the system even more money.

The changes offered here would create a system dramatically different from the way healthcare works today; the economics of such a shift would be profound, though not necessarily negative, for the medical industry. This idea of seeing doctors less frequently does sound odd. But think about your car: If it's running fine and the red light hasn't turned on, there's no need to see the mechanic. Well, we now have a red light – for you, not your car – and it's called remote monitoring.

Today, the system is overburdened. A classic example is just

---

[1] Nash, Esther, et al. "Is the 80/20 Rule of Health Care Still True? Deloitte United States, 14 May 2018, www2.deloitte.com/us/en/pages/life-sciences-and-health-care/articles/is-80-20-rule-of-health-care-still-true-population-value-based.html.

trying to get a new patient appointment for a chronic condition diagnosis, like hypertension. For the person who gets a high blood pressure reading at their local pharmacy, it takes a really long time to get into an open slot to see the doctor. And when their consultation does finally happen, they're told they are doing great – it must have been that low-salt diet and jogging they started since the high reading.

With a comprehensive system of remote monitoring in place, however, the medical centers would be able to prioritize and focus on those actually in need of hands-on medical attention. Everyone else would receive insightful and personally informed prompts and advice, keeping them both healthy and out of the system. And thanks to the data, we could predict even more, identifying individuals whose conditions will become more expensive to treat over time and guiding them to the appropriate care. Across the board, people would see measurable results and continue to use the system, financially rewarding it (and the patients, in money saved) for its effectiveness. This really is the promise of Livongo. The data we provide is less of a snapshot and more of a continuous movie about a member's health, an ever-evolving, 360-degree picture that anticipates needs and puts the member in charge and ultimately is able to pick up early signals of anything from kidney failure to heart disease to depression. This is the potential: true, meaningful, and actionable insights that improve the outcomes in people's lives.

67

## *Chapter Eight Summary: Health Versus Healthcare*

- Today's healthcare system is about helping patients get better when they are sick. Health is about empowering the person to create health for himself or herself and making it easier to stay healthy.

- People with chronic conditions are paying for the majority of a healthcare system that actually is not built around them or their needs, because the current system has the competing missions of care, revenue generation, and cost containment.

- The current medical system is opaque to the patient when it comes to fiscal accountability: real costs, costs in competitive practices, the correlation between quality and costs of providers.

- Remote monitoring gives us the power over time to anticipate needs and put the members more in charge.

# CHAPTER 9

# *The Livongo Model*

HEALTHCARE IS AMAZINGLY COMPLEX and personal and important. There is truly nothing like it. So it's not easy to build an effective and cohesive system that addresses the complete set of obstacles – from empowering people to better manage their diets to making it easier for them to get their test strips. If it were, someone in Silicon Valley would have already done so at the same time that others were growing game-changers like Twitter, Orbitz, Slack, and Square. Many tried it. And they failed.

Building a revolutionary healthcare system requires a bit of everything: timing, activated consumers, technology, a "we will try anything" mentality, and, of course, desperation in the industry.

The timing worked in Livongo's favor because the investment dollars had turned their eye to the vast opportunity in healthcare at the same time the various technologies had evolved to the point that they could network to provide one comprehensive picture.

So it was a good time to start, but where to start? Livongo was unlikely to start direct-to-consumer. People with chronic conditions were already overwhelmed with the three Cs (particularly cost), and there was no reasonable way to cut through the noise and make a compelling argument directly to that audience, at scale. Moreover, as frustrating and confusing as healthcare finance and insurance are, consumers have become trained to look for answers within the system (choosing in-network options) rather than forge into the uncharted – sticking with the devil you know, as they say.

When an innovative new healthcare company first brings its products to market, it needs customers. Large, self-insured employers are often on this cutting edge, as they directly benefit from improved overall experience, clinical outcomes, cost savings, and productivity. Insurance companies seem to be obvious options to deliver this, given their expansive reach, but in reality they are slow to move. Most insurance companies have innovation centers, where novel ideas spend years spinning without the ability to get to scale.

That's because large insurance companies are inherently actuarial, which means they focus on the risk as much as, if not more than, the opportunity. Actuarial models are run over tens of thousands of clients over multiple years of experience, measuring the potential downside against the upside. That explains why insurance companies are slower to adopt novel, innovative ideas.

In order to partner with health plans in a large-scale way, Livongo would have to earn a seat at that table. We would start by showing them how their own clients – large, self-insured companies – are frustrated and looking for answers outside the traditional industry players. Livongo would show, too, how the employees at these large companies are increasingly demanding the services we supply. Finally, Livongo would show how, by achieving improved clinical outcomes for those employees, the large, self-insured companies are racking up sizable savings from our services. That last point should get the attention of any health plan that's looking to increase its profit and performance.

## *The Power of the Self-Insured Employer*

The U.S. healthcare system divides care almost evenly between self-insured employers and Medicare and Medicaid.[1] Of the three, self-insured employers turned out to be the most fertile ground for Livongo, because they are traditionally the most innovative. They have two reasons to care about employee health: cost and productivity. According to the Gallup Well-Being report, health issues cost the U.S. $84 billion in absenteeism every year, and a stunning 77% of U.S. workers have at least one chronic condition, ranging from asthma to obesity.[2] Remember, too, that diabetes is a family disease, with employees often missing work because a family member is ill. According to *The Journal of Occupational and Environmental Medicine*, that cost in lost productivity is four times greater than the actual medical costs of treating the chronic conditions that caused it.[3]

So, we made our big bet. Approaching the self-insured companies, we said, "We have a way to make you and your employees happier and healthier and save money. Interested?" We explained that their employees would feel empowered because nothing was being dictated to them; they could choose to participate and be a member of Livongo; everything was voluntary (employees would "opt in" for services they wanted); the employer had to pay us only for employees who voluntarily signed on and regularly used the product; and when the member became healthier, this would lead to cost savings. It was

71

[1] "State Health Facts: Health Insurance Coverage of the Total Population." The Henry J. Kaiser Family Foundation, 2 Jan. 2019.
[2] Witters, Dan and Liu, Diana. "In U.S., Poor Health Tied to Big Losses for All Job Types." May 7, 2013 https://news.gallup.com/poll/162344/poor-health-tied-big-losses-job-types.aspx
[3] Goetzel, Ron Z., et al. "The Workforce Wellness Index." *Journal of Occupational and Environmental Medicine*, vol. 55, no. 3, Mar. 2013, pp. 272–279, doi:10.1097/jom.0b013e318278274e.

a narrative that a lot of companies understood right away – we could see the HR teams getting their finance people enthusiastically on board, quickly. If you want a healthy company, you do what you can to keep your employees healthy.

We knew we were going to have a hard time convincing companies to pay for this service unless we could prove that every investment they made would generate greater savings down the road. And we were able to prove exactly that. In year one, the average client realizes a 3.6 times return on investment and an average cost savings of $108 per person/per month.[4] In a cost-savings study of employees with diabetes at two large, self-insured companies comparing Livongo members with nonmembers, there was a medical cost decrease of 5%. (And if 5% seems small to you, I suggest you listen to the song "Seven and a Half Cents" from the Adler & Ross musical "The Pajama Game.")

Self-insured companies have a very pragmatic approach. They know who shows up healthy and who doesn't. In a way, they share the same self-interest the member does: Both want the member to be healthy, productive, and working. As Glen Tullman put it:

> We believe that market innovation is going to be driven by self-insured employers. That's exciting because they make decisions quickly. They are the payer, there's no intermediary. There are only three metrics:
> 1. Do our people love it?
> 2. Do you make them better and can you measure that?
> 3. Do you save money?[5]

Livongo hits all three metrics, and that is why we are growing at the

---

4 Livongo.com
5 (Tullman et al.)

rate we are growing.

Our initial commercial market orientation paid off. Companies like Pepsico, SAP, Target, and HP have signed on and are discovering the benefits of Livongo's services. Ultimately, though, we know that continued growth requires that we expand to government (Medicare and Medicaid) and insurance company sectors. Considering how bureaucratic these systems are, one might ask, why bother with them at all? We could keep finding large companies that want to make life better for their employees. Why move beyond that?

The answer comes back to our mission. We are not here to empower people with chronic conditions as long as they work at a Fortune 500 company. Rather, we are about empowering all people with chronic conditions. By connecting with the insurance plans, we will expand beyond the Fortune 500 companies to the smaller groups (those with fewer than five thousand, and especially fewer than three thousand, employees) that are the bread and butter of the health-plan industry. These groups include fully insured funding models, level funding, or minimum-premium models and often have stop-loss limits. More simply, with these groups the health plan has a bigger say in what benefits are packaged and how it rolls out to market. So, with our growing track record, the clinical outcomes, and financial savings in numbers that an actuary can understand, health plans have become key partners in our ongoing success.

73

## *Chapter Nine Summary: The Livongo Model*

- The timing was right to start Livongo, but where to begin?
  - Working with self-insured employers. Fertile ground for revenue opportunities:
    - Aligned incentives: Self-insured companies benefit directly from improved clinical outcomes in terms of cost savings and productivity. (If you want a healthy company, do what you can to keep your employees healthy.)
    - Immediate feedback: Self-insured companies know who shows up healthy and who doesn't, sharing the same self-interest the member does. (Both want the member to be healthy, productive, and working.)
  - Self-insured employers make decisions quickly. No intermediary. They have three simple metrics:
    - Do our people love it?
    - Can we make them measurably better?
    - Are we making/saving money?

    Livongo hits all three. And Livongo demonstrates cost savings: Our clients see a 3.6x ROI and $108 PPPM average cost savings in year one.

- Livongo is gaining traction in the government (Medicare and Medicaid) and the insurance company sectors.
  - This is important for our ongoing growth, as health plans will become key partners in our ongoing success.
  - More importantly, to be true to our mission, we are here to empower all people with chronic conditions.

# CHAPTER 10

## *Focus on the Whole Person*

ALL YOU HAVE TO DO is walk into a hospital and you can intuitively sense the problem. Every department is in a different part of the building, in another wing, on a separate floor. It's a maze, physically and metaphorically. The experts are isolated and feel disconnected. If you have a heart condition, diabetes, and are overweight, you might see a cardiologist, an endocrinologist, and a nutritionist. That's in addition to your general practitioner or internist and the coach assigned by your insurance company. Your labs are on yet another floor. And they might even give you conflicting advice. But all you really care about is the difficulty of dealing with all of your medical conditions, and frankly, that can make you feel pretty depressed. Every condition comes with its own feelings, and when people have multiple chronic conditions, they don't typically feel good. To think of anyone distinctly as a condition or in a silo is to compartmentalize and limit that person. And when you address people merely as a condition, many of the complexities and ramifications of those conditions can get lost.

It's not difficult to understand why the medical establishment has consistently avoided seeing the human condition more holistically. The original classification systems of Aristotle and Linnaeus encouraged a discipline of separation and specialization that, over the centuries, has increasingly disassociated and isolated our various conditions from one another, and from ourselves. Today, the pendulum is swinging back to a recognition that, just as the song tells us, the knee bone really is connected to the leg bone. In other words, systems and conditions – in our bodies and in the world – are inextricably conjoined. We understand now that the barriers between illnesses are often merely academic, and actually, by addressing them holistically, we can see better results.

The fact is that if you are going to take care of someone with diabetes, you need to care about more than just their blood glucose readings. You also need to care about blood pressure and lipids, because the majority of people with diabetes will see more medical problems from cardiovascular events than their diabetes.

Thankfully, the pendulum is swinging back on this aspect as well. Recent diabetes drugs are now being evaluated not only on their ability to reduce blood glucose levels, but also on their ability to drive cardiovascular outcomes. SGLT-2 inhibitors are beneficial not just for their ability for blood glucose control but also for reducing blood pressure. GLP-1 agonists are drugs that help with diabetes and also promote weight loss. Cardiologists are now finding themselves in a world where they need to stay abreast of diabetes drugs to optimize for cardiovascular outcomes.

But it is not just that people often have more than one chronic condition (we know 70% of our members with diabetes also have high blood pressure). It is that we need to think of each "patient" as a person (we call them members) and understand that person holisti-

76

cally. A patient's socioeconomic status may have as much to do with that patient's physical and mental health as any "clinical" metric. To truly optimize health for that individual, we have to consider it all, and yet, today, most of our physicians are neither trained to do so nor have the information to make that possible.

A quote from a Livongo coach, Sarah Hults, points to how we work with the whole person and the complexity that can come with multiple conditions:

> Most of our members don't just have diabetes. They may have hypertension or are overweight and on five or six medications. Our objective is to try to be understanding and positive and allow them to be vulnerable.

What she is describing is a level of individual complexity – one that a service limited to addressing merely one condition could never address.

## People Are 3-D

That same coach, Sarah, also has another perspective on interacting with a member – a completely different and fundamentally important perspective on what working with the whole person can mean:

> Some members are very happy when they get reached. Some members are just having a tough day and you have to meet them where they are. If they're having a tough day, we offer support ("What can I do for you?"). If they say nothing, then we back off. We don't want to push anyone.

We are there for them, and they are never alone.

This is the other side of treating the whole person, understanding that people don't live one-dimensional lives. Everyone has highs and lows. In order to positively affect people with chronic conditions, we quickly learned we had to connect with them across multiple touch points. Instead of focusing only on a clinical goal for one chronic condition, we needed to reach the whole person. If we didn't, the effectiveness of our work would continually run into roadblocks. In one instance, we were empowering a member to get his blood glucose values in a safe zone, but he continued to tag every reading with the "I don't feel good" option.

• • •

**We had to connect with people across multiple touch points, and we needed to reach the whole person.**

• • •

Note: At Livongo we are looking at not only blood glucose levels, but also how someone is feeling, what their eating patterns are, and a whole lot more. Even though his blood glucose readings improved, he still did not feel well. We nudged him to speak with one of our CDE (certified diabetes educator) coaches, and we learned that even though his blood glucose levels appeared in control, he still felt overwhelmed about the day-to-day responsibilities of living with his diabetes. So we needed to go beyond solely getting his blood glucose levels in check and offer psychological support and reassurance, even when (in fact, because) the clinical goal had been met. We needed to think about this member as a whole person, living with diabetes, not simply someone with diabetes with whom we were working to control blood glucose readings. When we treat people more holistically, appreciate them as so much more than a condition or (even worse) a symptom, and provide them with solutions they can understand and integrate into

78

their lives, we allow them to succeed on every front.

Empowerment requires creating a dialogue and consistent reinforcement. A system of cheering, nudging, and supportive encouragement that fosters positive motivation. In order to do this, we must utilize tools outside the healthcare system and even outside health – because in the end, people are not motivated merely (or even predominantly) by their health. So we need to think of people much more broadly, understanding what motivates and drives them, what they need, and what they care about.

Coming out of medical school, I was tempted to follow a path of becoming a practicing internist. Internists, which is the shortening of "internal doctor" (you could think of them as doctors focused on anything that might affect an adult), are the front line when it comes to understanding and empathizing with adult patients. They learn about their patients and, by motivating them with something they care about, get them to take actions that will optimize their health. For example, for patients who should exercise to lose weight, suggesting they build into their day time to take their dog for longer walks or spend quality time strolling with their spouses often drives better results than telling patients that to achieve clinical results they should walk more. All of this comes from ongoing communication, a deep understanding, and a common-sense approach.

A simple number shows the difference between the current system and what Livongo offers: 19.6[1] hours. A little less than a day. That's the average time devoted to education about nutrition in a student's med school career. It suffices to say that nutrition is not an area of particular expertise for the vast majority of doctors. But a comprehensive understanding of diet and nutrition is essential to managing diabetes and other chronic conditions, and proper nutrition could actually help turn those

[1] Adams, Kelly M., et al. "Nutrition Education in U.S. Medical Schools: Latest Update of a National Survey." *Academic Medicine*, vol. 85, no. 9, 2010, pp. 1537–1542., doi:10.1097/acm.0b013e3181eab71b.

conditions around. Knowing this, Livongo has built nutrition and life-style management as a core part of its offerings. Nearly 90% of Livongo CDEs are registered dietitians, certification for which – in addition to a bachelor's degree in nutrition or dietetics (typically) – 1,200 hours of supervised experience and passing a rigorous exam are required. This equips us with the ability to educate members every day with relevant advice and bite-size facts that make our members not only healthier, but more informed about how to better manage their condition through diet and nutrition.

Of course, from a business perspective, this opens the door to new offerings and opportunities. We have designed for and covered an increasing number of conditions, starting first where the overlap was biggest: From diabetes we went into hypertension, then into weight management, and, most recently, into behavioral health (depression, anxiety, sleep, substance abuse, pain). Each one of these conditions touches another, and our ability to empower members to manage all of them at the same time with one app, one coach, and one inte-grated whole-person approach improves their overall health. These expansions have been an important driver of our business growth, but more importantly, they have been an important driver in making our members happier and healthier.

## *Also, Design Matters*

A final aspect of the idea of the "whole person" that we always keep in mind is one of aesthetics. It may seem minor to some, con-sidering the gravity of the medical issues we manage, but we believe the ease and pleasure of an experience is tantamount to (and can be a key factor in) its efficacy. Simply put, form and function are equally important, and we believe that design thinking and user experience are critical to showing members how much we respect them.

The first and most important thing design can do is remove hassles. Imagine if every time you searched for something on Google you had to type in your password, and it was a separate password for every search. Google's usage would be dramatically reduced and its stock price would follow. We want Livongo to be as simple to use as looking up a movie on IMDB or getting Siri to give you directions to the nearest health food store.

For a real-world example closer to healthcare, take clinical thermometers. Until recently, they hadn't substantively changed since Daniel Gabriel Fahrenheit's first practical glass thermometer design in the early 1700s. The time needed to get an accurate, stable reading from one still remains difficult, requiring up to eleven minutes for a precise axillary (armpit) temperature measurement, eight minutes for oral, and five minutes for rectal temperature, often the most accurate (and discomforting) of the three. It's a sad but unsurprising irony that Fahrenheit himself died after a sudden bout of fever in 1736.

The 1964 invention of the noninvasive tympanic (ear) thermometer and, in the 1990s, the forehead thermometer completely changed the patient's experience of having their temperature taken and revolutionized our ability to quickly and accurately gauge a vital data point of a person's health. This is how you design an addictive product, by eliminating every obstacle between the user and what that user wants and needs. The way something looks and feels can have a profound effect on the way it works. And, not surprisingly, when made simple, the new thermometers quickly were adopted for home use.

We maintain just as high a standard on the devices Livongo provides, not just in how they're used, but from the moment our members first encounter them. Historically, the attention given to the packaging of medical devices has been on par with that for RadioShack's first

DIY computers: cheap, jumbled, and confusing ... all noise. Inspired by the level of holistic design that Jonathan Ive brought to Apple's computers and other hardware, we've been able to elevate an experience that was historically on the other end of the spectrum (thanks to the low bar set across most medical products) to something both functional and desirable.

One of our goals is to make the arrival of Livongo's monitoring devices and supplies a delightful experience. There may be no more flattering proof that we're on track than the "unboxing" moments we've seen posted on YouTube from members opening their blood pressure cuffs or blood glucose meters. The effort and expense we've taken to improve even this part of the experience is a way of our saying to every member, right out the gate: "You are valuable to us. We recognize you still have to stick a lancet into your finger to get a drop of blood, but we are sending you something more than just a generic box with a cheap disconnected meter in a flimsy case. We understand that parts of managing this condition get old very quickly, and we want this to be the beginning of an entirely new experience for you."

The city planner Maurice Cox once spoke about the purpose and importance of good architecture in constructing cities. When you build a beautiful library or police station or firehouse, he said, you make the citizens around it feel worthy of that beauty – they feel better about themselves and about their place in society. It's not just a building, it's a beacon of hope and promise and potential. This is what great design does. It is what Livongo tries to do with every investment we make in our products, whether it is a blood pressure monitor or blood glucose meter, or even just the cases that hold our devices. We know there is value beyond the pragmatic functionality, and we invest in it. We are honestly here to empower our members and make them feel great about themselves.

82

## *Chapter Ten Summary: Focus on the Whole Person*

- We do not think of people as conditions.

- People don't live one-dimensional lives, so Livongo approaches the whole person. By doing so we empower them to succeed on every front.
  - We have built out and covered multiple conditions, starting where there was the most overlap: diabetes, hypertension, weight management, behavioral health (depression, anxiety).
  - Coaching techniques expand across multiple touchpoints and conditions faced by people with chronic conditions.

- Livongo reaches beyond what the current system offers, providing nutrition and lifestyle management tools delivered by experts trained in those fields.

- A final aspect to seeing "the whole person," Livongo addresses aesthetics – providing well-designed, quality products and a better experience at every touch point, all of which tells the member, "You are valuable to us."

- These expansions have driven our business growth, but more importantly, they are important drivers in making our members healthier.

83

# CHAPTER 11

## *The Power of Curated Choice*

IF YOU LOOK at all the offerings out there, you would think people are clamoring for more – more choices, more lab values, more apps, and more devices. But it's a fallacy. We call it the Myth of More: the idea that more choices will magically help us do the things we need to do to manage our lives.

The billion-dollar business of SEO and search engine marketing is simple proof that, with very few exceptions, consumers actually don't want more choice. When Google first appeared, many of us would click through several screens of the results offered to ascertain what best suited our needs. But as Google's PageRank™ algorithm developed, we soon discovered that it was actually pretty good at prioritizing the most relevant results for our search terms. Over time, trust developed, and instead of scrolling through pages of search results, we can generally find what we are looking for within the first couple of choices offered (which explains the saying, "The loneliest place in the world is the second page of a Google search.")

Of course, with Google, we still need to remind ourselves to skip past the paid ads, because their business models rely on balancing intuitive learning with the need to generate revenue. So, along with curation, there's an element of trust that needs to be managed.

This balance is happening today in fashion as well, with wardrobe-styling companies like Stitch Fix, Trunk Club, and Wantable all working with the same basic model: Users are sent a box of clothes every month, keeping what they want to own and sending back the rest. Based on returns, the services get to know each member's preferences, improving their selections and take-rates, ultimately lowering costs and making their clientele look better on an ever-improving basis.

When it comes to an individual's medical care, there are also choices people want to make, but they are all upstream. "Who should be my primary care doctor?" "Who should be my child's pediatrician?" Yet even with these initial decisions, we want choice, but not too much. We need shortcuts. We do not want to have to peruse the entire directory of doctors in our area, or even scroll through the directory of local doctors covered by our insurance carrier. We'd rather just see the list of nearby doctors covered by our plan who can take care of people like us. Because what we would really like is to find a doc who would fit us or our families. That's why we normally ask friends and family for recommendations. It's not because we think they will know who the better doctor is, but rather because they know us better and will therefore know who would work best for the kind of person we are.

This is particularly exaggerated in the world of behavioral health, where, when looking at a psychiatrist or psychologist online, it is difficult to find one who specializes in the treatment we are seeking (now *that* is an industry prime for disruption). But once you have done your research and chosen your doctor, you want the experts to provide the guidance.

A first-hand illustration: When I was having my baby, after being in labor for more than a day, I was asked by the medical staff if I wanted a C-section. They wanted me to make a choice. After thirty hours of labor. I mean, *What?!* I practically screamed at them, "A choice? If I have to choose at this point in this agony, I'd rather not have a kid at all. Seriously, you're the experts, *you tell me.*"

The world of giving birth is one in which "empowering" women has become more standard. Women are now encouraged to create their own birth plans prior to delivering as a way to gain more voice and control in the situation. But the reality is that as things unfold, the situation frequently differs from the ideal, and what a delivering mom-to-be often wants is a series of "curated choices." Within their guiding principles (whatever those may be), they would like to choose from the best available options. For example, if the overriding preference is to not have any pain medications during the process, then the woman would like to have multiple options to manage pain that do not include medications. She wants a choice, but a curated choice within her parameters.

For me, delivering a baby as a person with type 1 diabetes (which automatically puts me in the high-risk category), the only set of curated options I wanted was to have a healthy baby. So, when I was presented with the "choice" of having a C-section (above and beyond having to consent for the surgery), I was overwhelmed. It would have been overwhelming even if I hadn't been exhausted from thirty hours of laboring. But I was in no place to actually make that decision. Especially since I perceived it to be outside of what I had already clearly communicated I wanted. I wanted a safe delivery, a healthy baby, and a healthy me. I was not the expert to pull that off. They were. And at that moment, being presented with that choice felt as though people were asking me whether a C-section was the way to achieve the outcomes I wanted. I had already made my choice when I chose the medical team to take care of me.

So, no, people do not want more choices. Life is complicated enough. And in the case of treating chronic conditions, more is definitely not better; it's worse. People with chronic conditions are already inundated with information to read, numbers to decode, medication to manage, devices to master. Instead of choices, people want accessible expertise. People want clear guidance. They want solutions that are personalized, timely, and actionable. And while we're at it, affordable. They want simplicity. One integrated system. One solution. And, please, make it easy, too. Just quiet the noise. Please.

The whole mission of our company is *empowerment*. This is why we never say that we "help" our members. Instead we prompt and nudge and are just there for our members when they need us. That's a different role from the historic responsibility of the medical assistant. This is why even the term "healthcare" seems slightly off. Yes, there are many people who do need capable and empathic caregivers attending to them, but there is a larger population of people (in fact, most of us) living with chronic conditions who are perfectly capable of taking care of ourselves. We all must be empowered to care for ourselves, while recognizing when we can benefit from support from a real live person. The idea that Livongo "cares" for its members borders on condescension – a dangerous trap the medical establishment has fallen into all too often.

We must build trust and rapport with our members to effectively provide them with a set of curated choices. This starts early in the process, when we invite them into our system. Here's a quick story from one of our members, talking about their work with their coach:

> We set up goals, and they started small at first. I'm going to check once a day, then try to move that up to twice a day,

and three times a day. I am going to take insulin on time. I'm going to take my pills on time. I'm going to start exercising, even though exercise is like a four-letter word to me. She knows me. Maybe more important, she understands me. And what would work for me.

Our success is based on how empathetic we can be. We use words that are encouraging and personalized to our members. For instance, on their first call, the coach may say something like, "I want to thank you for scheduling a coaching session today. I'm really excited to get to know you better so we can get into whatever you'd like to focus on." We talk about upcoming holidays, how it might be stressful for them, and we offer ways to allow them to achieve and accomplish their goals. It's about discovering the things they care about and offering up ways we can assist them in reaching those goals.

Once members are enrolled in our system, we reciprocate value through personalized nudges and recommendations each and every time they give us a blood glucose reading, followed up with curated choices like, "Would you like to enroll in a weight-loss service? This can get you to your blood glucose goals and give you more energy." Or, "Medications are expensive. Did you know that if you check your blood glucose level five times a month, your generic medications are covered for free?" Or, "We have a program to fine-tune the right dose of long-acting insulin, faster. We think it would be a great fit for you. Do you want to try?" Again, we are giving programs and choices to the individual, based off of what we know about them. So, choices, yes, but not the same standard menu for everyone. Curated first, based on our expertise, and then personalized to the member, based on what they've shared and what we've learned works for them. Just like Amazon or Netflix recommending a book or movie for you.

While some innovations in this field promote the idea of giving people with diabetes the opportunity to be more engaged in maintaining their health, we are actually happy if they're *less* engaged – if the tools and prompts we give them make managing their chronic conditions more automatic, it simply becomes a reflexive part of their lives. Our belief is that people, consciously or subconsciously, are already overwhelmed, which is another way of saying that they're emotionally *too engaged* with their diabetes. Our job is to make it all easier.

It is not all nudging and prompts. Our coaches have also found that simply acknowledging accomplishments, no matter how big or how small, keeps people moving forward. To quote Livongo coach Morgan Robbins:

> A lot of times people think, if it's not perfect, it's not right. So, getting positive affirmation for even small accomplishments, like adding more vegetables to their diet, helps them realize that they are on a journey, that small steps lead to bigger successes.

If a coach has not heard from a member for a couple of weeks and the data shows that member does want to be tracking their condition, we might reach out with a message like, "Hey, Rachel, now's a great time to hop on and log three meals by the end of the week." Or, "Hi, John. Are you up for a challenge of logging twelve thousand steps each day for the rest of the week? Let's see if you can make it happen." Our experience shows that a simple, nonjudgmental reminder, a kind of quick, short nudge, often puts a member back into action, inspiring a response like, "Oh, yeah! I totally forgot! Let me get back to this." As Jesse Bridgewater, our Vice President of data science, said:

All of our members get digitally coached with every interaction, and these digital messages are personal and very tailored. When a message gets a really good response, our reinforcement learning platform knows to send that one out again to similar people. We get smarter every time we send a message.

We've also developed a disengaged-member protocol with milestones that measure the member's level of utilization. We can see when a member is syncing their weight or watching a lesson, and of course we know if they are communicating with us. If they're not doing any of those things and they are not reaching out to us, our disempowered-member protocol kicks in. It begins with sending a weekly tip. It might be about nutrition, or mindset, or exercise. It's designed to give this member space but let them know that we are not giving up on them. We want them to know that their coach is there if or when they're ready and want to come back.

We constantly try to find ways to meet the members where they are – it's a strategy that works and, we think, sets us apart.

90

# *Chapter Eleven Summary: The Power of Curated Choice*

- The Myth of More leads us to the idea that people whose lives are complicated by chronic conditions don't want a lot of choices; they want to choose from the best available options – a curated choice – accessible expertise; clear guidance; and actionable, personalized solutions that are timely, easy, and affordable.

- We empower our members through nudges, encouragement, and recommendations – curated choices based on:
  - Our expertise,
  - What they've shared, and
  - What we've learned.

- We know we have done our job of empowering people when the tools we give them make managing their health so automatic that they become less engaged with their condition.

- Meeting members where they are is a key strategy.

91

# CHAPTER 12

## *Invent It, Name It*

BACK IN 1897, the Otis Elevator Company had a new invention. Its founder, Elisha Otis, had revolutionized urban design with his safety elevator almost fifty years earlier. Its new invention revisited that original notion, but with a twist: It was based on a staircase. Borrowing from its original idea and merging it with the Latin term for "step" (*"scala"*), the company coined the term "escalator." And invented an entire category. It was so novel (shocking, in fact) that customers had to be "revived with smelling salts and cognac" after their first time riding it. Today, the escalator is as common as Scotch tape, kitty litter, and bubble wrap – all original names for innovations that eventually became part of our everyday language. New ideas demand a flexibility from our lexicon, and as a species, we have proved incredibly accommodating at allowing in these novel terms. (You can Google it.) Perhaps this is a clue to our remarkable ability to evolve, innovate, and articulate.

There was a time when Livongo itself was struggling for language. As we began to mature, we were being asked questions like,

"What are you? Are you a device company?" Well, we do have cool connected devices, but we're more than that. "Are you a diabetes company?" We *do* work with more than 150,000 people with diabetes, but we're more than that. "Are you a coaching company?" Well, we have more than one hundred highly qualified and empathetic coaches, but we're more than that. "A data science company?" Yes, we may soon have more data scientists than developers, which would be very unique in Silicon Valley. But (you guessed it) we're more than that. We were doing something new, and it didn't neatly fit into any existing paradigm. So, yes, we were all of these, yet none of these singularly. We were building and delivering an experience for people with chronic conditions that generated unheard-of net promoter scores in the healthcare world. We drove sustainable clinical outcomes and provided measurable cost savings to the entire system. We were addressing the three Cs (confusion, complexity, and cost) head-on and silencing the noise in the healthcare system. So, we gave this "experience" that we created a new name. We called it Applied Health Signals.™

As a term, it is pretty simple. No fancy Latin folded into the phrase, no clever portmanteau like "styrofoam" (which, technically, is really "closed-cell extruded polystyrene foam"). But the term "Applied Health Signals" does concisely describe what we do. At a basic level, we gather Health Signals from your body and deliver them back to you at the exact right moment. But to do that isn't so easy. A more technical description is that it is a sophisticated system built by a constant, informed, and dynamic engine that, we believe, will drive revolutionary change in care. Powered by our AI+AI™ engine (which stands for Aggregate, Interpret, Apply, and Iterate), Applied Health Signals are accurate, actionable, and personalized insights and support, delivered to members when they need it most. Thanks to this system, by combining multiple data sets from Livongo devices, apps, coaches, and a host of other sources – we get better at making people better every day. AI+AI doesn't just make us smarter every day, it makes us more effective, understanding, and empathetic. The key elements are easy to grasp:

***Aggregate:*** *We'll take data from anywhere and get it from everywhere.*

Health data comes into Livongo in a variety of ways. Some of that data is collected in real time from our own connected Livongo devices, including blood glucose values, blood pressure values, weight, body composition, meal timing, mental health state, and much more. Data can also come from our own coaches inputting information into the Livongo Applied Health Signals engine. Other data that we aggregate and use to build signals includes gender, age, zip code, and responses to the Diabetes Empowerment Scale survey or other psychographic survey data. It's also pulled from our partners' devices, like Abbott's Freestyle Libre Continuous Glucose Monitor, and from traditional data sources, like medical claims or Electronic Health Records (EHR) – we have a long-term strategic relationship with Cerner, the largest and leading provider, and other EHRs. We even receive input from partner application programming interfaces (APIs), like nutritional data or Apple's HealthKit.

All of these inputs get aggregated into the Applied Health Signals engine, where we create more than data – we create signals. By normalizing these inputs for usability, we dimensionalize the signals to ascertain which ones are the most meaningful for a specific use, establish key models to use the signals, and develop our entirely new class of Livongo proprietary signals.

## *Interpret:* What's it all mean?

Next, our data scientists assess the signals. We take what we know about the individual (gathered from our devices, coaches, prompts, etc.), combine it with a host of additional data streams (behavioral, geographical, socioeconomic data, etc.), and interpret it all to find unique combinations that can be applied for behavior change with members. This includes not just the most relevant healthcare message (which is often tricky to identify across conditions), but – equally, if not more importantly – where to deliver this information, through which communication channel (e.g., text message, phone call). Along with the words and language we should use that will best motivate that individual to take the desired action. As part of that effort, our team of data scientists, behavior specialists, and clinicians work on specific signals for individual conditions as well as across conditions. This work also includes determining which applications are most appropriate for which output signals for which members.

## *Apply:* Delivering the right information at exactly the right time.

Here we look at a broad set of ways we apply signals to specific people for a specific action and behavior support at the right time. We don't just think of applications the way apps on a smartphone do things. We think of these as the channels through which signals are transmitted to key stakeholders. Examples of Livongo applications include Health Nudges™ delivered through the blood glucose meter or mobile app; using specific modalities for a specific member targeting for enrollment; community engagement; voice-based coaching guidance; and free medications coordinated through our pharmacy and PBM partners. Applications can be for our members, for other stakeholders

95

in the healthcare ecosystem (like providers or clinicians), or even for family members. They could be applications that provide signals to a provider's scheduling system that tell them when an individual needs an outbound telehealth call, or even governmental applications to support people on SNAP food programs.

Apply, as a process, is still at its early stages, and we are investing heavily here. Over time you can imagine a marketplace where Livongo supports applications and services from third parties that can be accessed by our members – offered to them as curated choices – to help solve different problems. Livongo's ability to interpret signals helps us match the right applications to members at the right time.

**Iterate:** *We get smarter as we see what works.*

As we present signals through a variety of applications, we activate feedback loops on what is valuable to shape the specific desired behavior change. For example, what type of message or nudge works best for a given individual? At what time of the day or what day of the week? What specific offerings (free medications, nutrition support, healthy meals) are most useful in actually improving their health? Those feedback loops iterate back into the engine to make each interaction higher value and higher impact.

The idea that the size and scale of data can improve service to customers is hardly new in the tech space – it started way back with Amazon's "People who liked *Lord of the Rings* also liked *Game of Thrones.*" Instagram, Netflix, and a host of consumer sites use similar tools. Livongo, using our AI+AI engine, is the first to effectively apply this thinking to chronic conditions. It makes sense that it has taken a bit longer to enter the healthcare space because ours needs tto be smarter, more personalized, and safer. After all, we're not just recommending a funny sitcom or a traffic-free backroad. We're providing suggestions, prompts, and support for people's health – things that can meaningfully better their lives.

Of course, considering the size of the business opportunity, it's no surprise that other companies are working with data in ways that resemble the AI+AI sphere. Artificial intelligence, in its truest form, should actually contain all four pillars. Unfortunately, in their rush to "get one of those AI things," companies are taking shortcuts, calling everything AI, even if it's simply a buzzword to help senior management feel as though their company isn't getting left in their competitors' dust. And the need for real AI in healthcare exists because the current AI companies do some but not all four of these pillars.

For example, IBM Watson aggregates and interprets really well but has no true "apply" capability, and therefore cannot iterate on its own – it's completely reliant on other parties, and thus can't close its own feedback loops. And many of the newest consumer technologies like wearable fitness trackers do a good job at iterating and applying along one dimension of data, such as steps, but they do not aggregate or interpret additional points of data that could be useful in motivating behaviors. Worse, there's no standard for reliability, and if they're getting false-positive results, they can potentially cause more harm than good because people start to ignore other signals. Additionally, because they don't provide any system to manage outcomes, those false positives often head straight into the already overcrowded hospitals.

Writing about the Apple Watch's heart monitor in a *New York Times* blog last fall, Dr. Aaron E. Carroll pointed out, "The healthcare system is already busy, if not overloaded. No physician wants to field calls from patients who have no problems. Such patients will require visits and further testing and will potentially receive interventions.

---

[1] Carroll, Aaron E. "That New Apple Watch EKG Feature? There Are More Downs Than Ups." *NYT: The Upshot, New York Times*, 8 Oct. 2018, www.nytimes.com/2018/10/08/upshot/apple-watch-heart-monitor-ekg.html.

They'll generate bills and harms without benefits."[1] It seems unusual that the Apple team didn't think that through, given their typical thoroughness. They were likely focused on the killer app – a cool Dick Tracy-style heart monitor watch (you can just imagine the whole team going "Ohhh." Because it *is* cool.) – when they should have also been considering how it fit into a complete system. It's also why pure tech companies from Silicon Valley have not been successful in health. First, they get enthralled with the technology, while their customers want solutions and answers. Second, they don't understand the typical workflows in healthcare. And, finally, unlike the consumer world, there is generally not a connection between who's paying for the service (or device) and who's benefiting.

Livongo's AI+AI engine helps us optimize people's health on multiple fronts. It helps optimize medications by combining up-to-date clinical status with medication tracking through tight partnerships with pharmacists from leading national chains. It provides smarter coaching for weight management by offering a broad program based on each individual's specific needs, preferences, and progress. It's built on psychographic targeting aimed at understanding a person's personality profile. And because people sometimes have a hard time paying for their medications, we can track and incentivize activities – such as regular blood pressure measurements – that will ensure the member can take advantage of copay programs that are enabled for certain medications.

Describing Applied Health Signals can all sound very academic and clinical. Here is how Holly Lemmons, a Livongo coach, describes our system in action for a member:

> First, working with the member, we set up strategy. I'm interpreting their data that's coming back subjectively in

the form of their feedback, or objectively in the form of their step count or weight data. Then we assess that in real time during our sessions and modify the approach based on what is or isn't working. Let's try something new, or let's step it up and keep rolling with it.

While the process of application and iteration Holly describes here is a blend of automated and human judgments, as we progress and gather more data, it escalates into more of an AI functionality. (Lucky break: Had Otis never invented the escalator and the term "escalate," we'd have had to use a less descriptive word there.)

Clearly, as we further develop Applied Health Signals and the AI+AI supporting it, there is great promise in applications that reach not only our members, but other stakeholders within the healthcare ecosystem. There could be applications that send signals to a clinician's scheduling system to tell them when a patient needs an outbound telehealth call or free medications. Additionally, we foresee applications that send messages to family members or even governmental applications to support people on SNAP food programs with nutrition support and healthy meal options.

We are at the early stages of investing in and developing these applications. But we see virtually endless possibilities. Applied Health Signals promises to free people with chronic conditions from the trap of noisy healthcare, empowering them with smart, personalized health choices that remove confusion, complexity, and cost.

The only way we will win in the long term is if our members feel as though we are an honest broker for them. Luckily, the flywheel of the AI+AI engine provides some insurance for us. Through Applied Health Signals, we will get to know and serve the customer better, in a more personalized and tailored fashion, creating a relationship with

99

the Livongo brand that will be increasingly difficult for a competitor to displace.

For contrast, look at the telehealth industry. Valued at $6 billion annually a few years ago, it's now projected to reach almost $20 billion by 2025. What's behind that growth? Frankly, the consumer is doing a workaround the current healthcare system. By letting the patient call a physician on demand, instead of going all the way to the doctor's office, telehealth creates efficiency and, ergo, value. It is a quick solution for acute, nonemergent needs (a sore throat, a UTI, a pimple, a refill for meds) and an effective tool for those already in control and empowered. But for the person with a chronic condition, because they are transactional by nature, telehealth solutions are not positive and empowering drivers of behavior change. Also – and this is a key distinction – they're not judged by clinical outcomes. Lastly, they don't have the depth of an ongoing two-way relationship: There's no real dialogue and only limited information, making it nearly impossible to build up trust in the telehealth system.

Once the market understands the power of AI+AI, it will inevitably encourage other brands to start developing their own systems that provide feedback loops and virtuous circles, supporting all sorts of conditions. The personalized insights and depth of knowledge that Applied Health Signals give us can transform our entire approach to health, improving clinical outcomes across the board.

We expect and welcome the day when other brands will also leverage AI+AI, and it's one reason why we identified Applied Health Signals as a category. Healthcare is a big problem to solve, and there's a lot of room here to do well (business-wise) by doing good (health-wise).

## *Chapter Twelve Summary : Invent It, Name It*

- When Livongo was created, we did not fit into any paradigm that existed, so we had to create our own category, Applied Health Signals, a name that defines an informed and dynamic engine that will drive revolutionary change in care.
  - Powered by our AI+AI engine (Aggregate, Interpret, Apply, and Iterate), Applied Health Signals are accurate, actionable, and personalized insights and support, delivered to members when they need it most.
  - By combining multiple data sets from Livongo devices, apps, coaches, and other sources, we get better and faster at making people better.
  - AI+AI not only makes us smarter every day, it makes us more effective, understanding, and empathetic.

101

- As we further develop Applied Health Signals, there is great promise in applications that reach not only our members, but other stakeholders within the healthcare ecosystem: clinicians, family members, and government agencies. We see endless possibility.

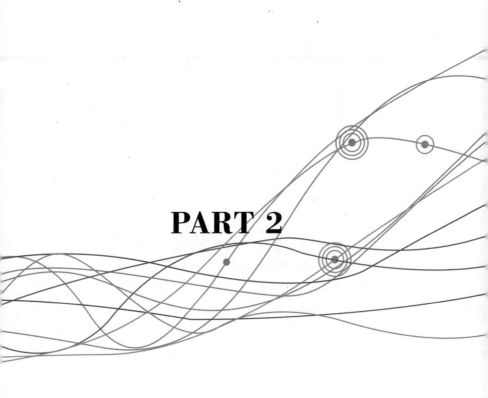

# PART 2

# CHAPTER 13

## *Growing Smarter*

THE FIRST PART OF THIS BOOK focused on why Livongo was built, what the opportunities were, and how we addressed them. Now I'd like to lean into how Livongo is building itself, what our principles and values are, and how we plan to grow. This is not intended to be a self-aggrandizing, chest-beating list of wins and kills. In fact, what I hope to demonstrate is that – in a Silicon Valley culture that still too often finds itself lavishly celebrating greed and unprincipled growth – we are working to live our values in a way that provides a model for ethical and sustainable stewardship.

Livongo has already gained momentum. We are building an SaaS (Software as a Service – think Office 365, Shopify, MailChimp) Applied Health Signals company with more than eight hundred customers and 350,000 members* across multiple products to assist with a variety of conditions.

The question is, are we just impressively growing the business, or are we also growing smarter? Fortunately, growing smarter is built into

---

*At the time of publication.

our business and product designs, the virtuous loop that is constantly learning – gaining insights, efficiency, and savings every cycle. Every day, high usage is providing more data and more productive feedback into the system, not only about one specific condition, but truly across the whole person. The insights we gain from delivering effective health signals to our members link us to learnings that allow us to empower a wider range of people across a growing set of solutions.

Let's put it into industry terms. In the SaaS model, companies sell one seat per user. Because so many of our users have other chronic conditions, the data is not only helping us deliver better advice and products across a range of conditions, it's also allowing us to sell multiple seats, for diabetes, hypertension, and depression. Again, doing well by doing good.

Someone once said, "The business of Amazon is to make more Amazon." It is a way of saying that once you have designed a business that seamlessly serves up anything a customer needs, the only limit to growth is how much any customer needs. In Amazon's case, it has yet to discover that limit. Livongo is looking at a similarly limitless horizon. Our members need actionable, personalized, and timely insights delivered at the right moment in the right way, across a wide variety of chronic conditions. As our membership grows and matures

• • •

**While we'll always be customer-focused, the business of Livongo is to make more Livongo.**

• • •

over time and we cover more conditions, the business of Livongo is to make more Livongo: coming up with more tools and prompts, empowering more and more members to live better and healthier lives, and cutting healthcare costs along the way, until that promising day when chronic conditions no longer exist.

Currently, we are saving our clients an average of about $108 a month for every employee with diabetes. Apply that number to the 180 million Americans with chronic conditions and it's easy to see a potentially huge economic impact. Is it too ambitious to believe we could add value to every person living with a chronic condition today? Perhaps. But let's see.

Glen Tullman often says, "Innovation begins by doing something new." Our challenges will grow as we expand, and we will constantly need to turn data into signals – actionable insights for our members. This is exciting. To date, no healthcare company has used the fundamental principles that empower consumers in the same way that other internet companies have across every other industry. Healthcare has been too busy trying to fix itself instead of reimaging, reinventing, and redesigning. It's as if the industry is busy trying to fix Kodak when the whole world is waiting for Instagram.

106

## Chapter Thirteen Summary: Growing Smarter

In Part 1, we focused on the why Livongo was built, what the opportunities were, and how we addressed them.

In Part 2, we focus how Livongo is building itself, what our principles and values are, and how we plan to grow going forward.

- We are a Software as a Service (SaaS) company that is experiencing robust growth.

- Our iteration of Health Signals lets us grow smarter, letting us serve members more effectively every day.

- We can serve more members with more conditions, promising better service and more growth.

107

- Livongo saves clients an average of $108 a month for every employee with diabetes. And that is just one condition we help with. Multiply that dollar amount by the 180 million Americans with chronic conditions and the resulting potential savings for clients could be huge.

- We are bringing something different to the industry: the insights, technology, and systems of a true customer-centered business.

# CHAPTER 14

## *Addressing Diversity*

RIGHT NOW, IN EVERY CORNER of our society, diversity matters more than ever. And it should. Diversity matters from 1) a business perspective, 2) a product-design perspective, and 3) a social-justice perspective.

From a business perspective, of course, it's common sense. Would you ever make a decision to exclude over half the market? Not only do we need to consider the whole market, we need to embrace it, reflect it, and provide leadership around the issue in every aspect of our organization. Considering that 50.8% of people in the U.S. are women, 18.1% are Hispanic, and 13.4% are African-American,[1] any new healthcare company, beginning with its board, its leadership, and its entire team, should reflect our entire society. And we are working to make that happen at Livongo.

Also, as a company built around empathy, we have to truly understand diversity if we are going to effectively speak with our members so that it interests, involves, and delights them in a way that

---

[1] "U.S. Census Bureau Quickfacts: UNITED STATES". *Census Bureau Quickfacts*, 2019, https://www.census.gov/quickfacts/fact/table/US/IPE120217.

empowers optimal outcomes. The landscape is only growing richer and more diverse, and in the decades to come, our AI+AI engine will learn the nuances of every culture with whom we engage. Considering our ambitions, being anything less than wholly open to this great opportunity would be curbing our own effectiveness.

Finally, we need to work on diversity simply to address the real issues of social justice that still weigh all too heavily on our business, culture, and society. We believe that to build a great company, not just a good one, you often have to consider more than just business. Doing the right thing keeps our best employees inspired and proud. And it's the right thing to do. As Hemant Taneja pointed out in a recent *Harvard Business Review* article, in 2018 a meager 13% of venture capital flowed to minorities, despite the fact that we live in a country where, as of the last census, 35% of businesses are owned by women and 28% are owned by minorities. For us to create a responsible, thriving, and healthy business, addressing this disparity needs to be folded into our daily business life. Diversity needs to inform our organization's perspective on hiring, partners, suppliers, alliances, and every other aspect of the work we do.

When we look at serving our members, we know that the female in most households serves as the "chief medical officer," making 80% of all healthcare decisions for the family.[2] Women also use the healthcare system more, in part because of their need for reproductive services. A study by the Centers for Disease Control and Prevention found that women are 33% more likely than men to see a doctor and twice as likely to use preventive services and get annual checkups. When it comes to cost, women ages 19 to 44 incur 80% higher costs than men in the same age range.[3]

---

[2] Stone, Terry. "New Report: Women Make 80% Of Buying Decisions But Represent Only 13% Of CEOs." *Oliver Wyman Health*, 9 Jan. 2019, health.oliverwyman.com/2019/01/women-in-healthcare-make-80--of-purchasing-decisions--yet-13--of.html.

[3] "General Facts on Women and Job Based Health," U.S. Department of Labor - Employee Benefits Security Administration, www.dol.gov/sites/default/files/ebsa/about-ebsa/our-activities/resource-center/fact-sheets/women-and-job-based-health.pdf.

However, women who work full time make less than men. White women bring home about 77% of the income earned by white men, on average. That percentage skews even lower for Hispanic and African-American women (53% and 66%, respectively).[4] And because women are most often the family's caretaker, they tend to take more time off to care for children, further reducing income.

When it comes to minorities as consumers, we know that these populations are hit much harder by chronic conditions. And whether it be from language and cultural barriers, lack of access to preventive care, or economic circumstances, many minority communities in this country do not receive adequate treatment under the current healthcare system. Compared with the general population, Hispanics have higher obesity rates.[5] Puerto Ricans suffer disproportionately from asthma.[6] And African-Americans, who are almost twice as likely to be diagnosed with diabetes as non-Hispanic whites, are also more likely to face limb amputation and develop kidney disease.[7] High blood pressure is also a large issue for African-Americans, who tend to develop it earlier in life, with numbers rising to much higher levels.[8]

**• • •**

**Doing well by doing the obvious.**

**• • •**

As long as there are significant – or even measurable – disparities in the quality and accessibility of care in marginalized communities, we have a responsibility to hold ourselves and our colleagues accountable in advocating for and providing culturally competent care that recognizes the needs of these (and all) communities. And we need

110

[4] (General Facts on Women and Job Based Health)
[5] "Obesity & Hispanics". Minorityhealth.HHS.gov, 2019, https://minorityhealth.hhs.gov/omh/browse.aspx?lvl=4&lvlid=70.
[6] Szentpetery, Sylvia E., et al" "Asthma in Puerto Ricans: Lessons from a high-risk population." *Journal of Allergy and Clinical Immunology*, vol. 138, 6, 2016, pp. 1156-1158.
[7] "Office of Minority Health." *Diabetes & African Americans*, 13 July 2016, minorityhealth.hhs.gov/omh/browse.aspx-?lvl=4&lvlid=18.
[8] "High Blood Pressure and African Americans." *American Heart Association*, 31 Oct. 2016, www.heart.org/en/health-topics/high-blood-pressure/why-high-blood-pressure-is-a-silent-killer/high-blood-pressure-and-african-americans.
[9] "Delivering Through Diversity." McKinsey & Company, Jan. 2018, www.mckinsey.com/business-functions/organization/our-insights/delivering-through-diversity.

solutions that are affordable in these communities.

When hiring within our organization, we know that it will serve us well to consider diversity and inclusion if we want a competitive advantage in the marketplace. A report from the management consulting firm McKinsey tells us that there is a link between diversity (defined as "a greater proportion of women and a more mixed ethnic and cultural composition in the leadership") and a company's financial performance.[9] McKinsey found that companies that rank in the top 25% for gender diversity on leadership teams were 21% more likely to experience "above average" profitability than the bottom quarter. It also found that ethnic diversity in the top quarter made a company 33% more likely to have above-average profitability than those companies in the bottom quarter. The report shows that diverse teams exceed more-homogeneous ones in terms of performance, talent, and employee satisfaction. This isn't about "doing well by doing good" anymore, but more like "doing well by doing the obvious."

For Livongo, diverse hiring connects directly back to the idea of keeping our members at the center of everything. When we have the ability to relate to and see the world through the eyes of our enormously wide variety of members, we are able to serve them far better. And in healthcare nothing is more important.

---

[9] "Delivering Through Diversity." McKinsey & Company, Jan. 2018, www.mckinsey.com/business-functions/organization/our-insights/delivering-through-diversity.

## *Chapter Fourteen Summary: Addressing Diversity*

- Diversity matters from a common-sense business perspective, especially for a company based on principles of empathy.

- It makes logical business sense to speak to as large an audience as possible, so embracing diversity is critical.

- You can't be truly empathetic to a wide customer base without making diversity a key element in your offering.

- Diversity matters from a perspective of social justice. We will never fix the inequalities present in our systems unless we work to address them in our business.

- In terms of building a strong, effective team:
  - Hiring with diversity and inclusion in mind will give us a competitive advantage in the marketplace.
  - Diverse teams outperform in talent and employee satisfaction.
  - Diverse hiring connects to the idea of keeping our members at the center of everything – innate understanding helps us serve them better.

# CHAPTER 15

# *Betting on the Culture*

THE RELATIVELY RECENT Amazon/Berkshire Hathaway/ JPMorgan Chase healthcare venture was created because, as Berkshire chairman Warren Buffett said, healthcare costs are "a hungry tapeworm on the American economy."[1] A fitting and graphic metaphor. Each one of these companies had lost confidence in the entire healthcare system – payers, PBMs, and hospitals – to drive higher quality and lower cost and act in the best interest of its customers. These companies wanted to create their own system "free from profit-making incentives and constraints." So they joined efforts and created a nonprofit with the aim of finding ways to increase satisfaction, improve the quality of healthcare offerings inside their companies, and cut costs. Even if all they do is accomplish their objective for their own employees, it would be impressive, as the three companies together employ 950,000[2] people worldwide.

The company leaders openly state that they know they faced

---

[1] LaVito, Angelica, and Jeff Cox. "Amazon, Berkshire and JPMorgan Chase to Team in Landmark New Health Care Company." *CNBC*, 30 Jan. 2018, www.cnbc.com/2018/01/30/amazon-berkshire-hathaway-and-jpmorgan-chase-to-partner-on-us-employee-health-care.html.
[2] (LaVito, 2018)

complexity and a high degree of difficulty as they attempt to navigate the world of healthcare. So they brought in the expertise of Dr. Atul Gawande, naming him CEO. Dr. Gawande is an amazing doctor with impeccable credentials. Yet hiring senior-level doctors from within the system has not historically proved to be the fastest path to innovation. It is my sincere hope that the marriage of his prowess paired with Jack Stoddard, who has a great entrepreneurial operating reputation, and their collective DNA of transformative change will bring about a whole new approach to healthcare.

I can tell you as a doctor, though, that we are not necessarily bred or trained for innovation. Doctors are trained to follow consistent rules. To practice evidence-based medicine. People want doctors to have clear-cut answers, and doctors take that to heart. We tread carefully around anything new (the threat of malpractice encourages, even ne-cessitates, that). As a result, doctors are more comfortable with the tried-and-true, the well-tested, the scientifically proven.

> • • •
> ## We can't solve problems by using the same kind of thinking that created them.
> • • •

As a nonpracticing doc, I have already stepped outside the norm, working in entrepreneurial environments, enjoying the freedom to use my training in a variety of ways to empower more people at scale, and embracing even tougher challenges. And with a team of smart folks around me, I have gravitated toward the blending of the medical and entrepreneurial, just as Livongo has fused together healthcare knowledge with the consumer-tech focus of Silicon Valley. Also, I credit Stanford University for a unique education that strongly em-phasized cross-pollination across disciplines and fields of study. This encourages me to weigh trade-offs in consumer demands versus the established healthcare conventions. Now, every day, I am pushed by

114

the diverse team we've assembled to create something new.

The well-worn (and, in fact, misattributed) Einstein quote "We can't solve problems by using the same kind of thinking that created them" fits well in this discussion. Change is hard. Change requires disruption. When you bring in doctors, healthcare administrators, and like-minded medical professionals and ask them how to change the system, you are unlikely to get very far. I see from the people I'm fortunate enough to have around me now that it takes expertise from varied disciplines to create a truly new type of magic.

It is diversity in experience, thinking, and points of view; challenging norms; and playing devil's advocate that is changing the current system. It's this approach that has allowed us the success we are currently seeing. And I believe it will continue to help us innovate and improve the system as we move forward. It starts with a great team.

## Team

Healthcare is complicated and challenging. That is in large part what makes it so rewarding. And why it attracts so many intelligent people to try to solve its problems. Which means I get to work with incredibly bright, driven people, every day. We have a special mix of people at Livongo, and it is inspiring how we have come to work together.

So many companies in Silicon Valley work to codify their culture, programming it in the same way they code their apps and search engines, expecting the same positive outcomes. They give unlimited PTO and put air hockey tables in the hallway. But their people are still miserable. I know, because I hire people fleeing from those companies on a weekly basis.

It's difficult to write about these things without sounding idealistic or overly simplistic. Yet the principles that define an effective and healthy culture are the rules we learn very early on, not just in our careers but in life. It's no wonder Robert Fulghum was able to make a *New York Times* best-seller from the thought "All I really need to know I learned in kindergarten." Play fair, share everything, clean up your own mess. These aren't soaring-eagle motivational posters you frame and hang in conference rooms. They're practical standards you hold yourself to every single day.

All too often, companies obsessed with finding the smartest and most accomplished person for the job – the proverbial rock star – wind up with a fractured culture of clashing egos, dueling agendas, and swollen payrolls. Not exactly a recipe for success. Just like in our product offering, our hiring looks to balance the IQ with the EQ, bringing together a wide range of talents, who, by working together, add up to an organization where the whole truly is greater than the sum of its parts.

So instead of hiring outside rock stars, we celebrate the stars in our midst. We recently did an executive team exercise where each member submitted one- to two-word phrases that best summed up the "superpowers" of each of their counterparts (truly believing, like the Avengers, that the sum is better than its parts). We then made superhero capes for each person with the words used to describe them. Some of the favorites included JediMindTrickster, Captain America, Scheherazade, The Plumber, Eidetic Memory, and Shapeshifter. It may be a corny, silly example, but it underscores a vitally important point: You can save your company a lot of money and spare a lot of egomaniacal nonsense if you focus on finding and nurturing the hidden strengths that are already on board.

We're also lucky that having a healthy culture and a successful company translates to very low turnover. Which means that instead of constantly onboarding and training new staff, our veteran sales teams can focus on deepening the relationships between our clients, adding to our overall stability and strength. That said, our fast growth does have us bringing in a lot of new people, with the average tenure now at six months. Moving at the rate we are going, we have to spend as much time worrying about cultural fit as CV qualifications. We take chances with our hires and look to see who can lead, who can keep up, and who is falling behind. To date, we've had some brilliant hires and real mismatches. I've discovered that one of the best things to do when you're running at such a fevered pace is to recognize when people just don't fit within the culture and do something about it as quickly as possible. In the end, everyone is healthier for it, even the folks who go their separate ways. It's all about fit. It's not that a person is good or bad, but rather that we know whether they fit or not. We want to be awesome at helping everyone at Livongo find a place where they can be successful.

> • • •
> **Play is the highest form of research.**
> • • •

117

## *Play*

As a mission-driven company, we all take our jobs incredibly seriously. But we do not take *ourselves* too seriously. We embrace another Einstein misquotation: "Play is the highest form of research." It was actually said by Neville Scarfe, who made a thought expressed by Einstein much pithier. And they were both right. It's how we discover who we really are. As a team, we have nicknames, sing parody songs with our own lyrics, and keep a running quote book of silly phrases and missteps. If you attend one of our board of directors meetings, it is advisable to look before you sit to avoid whoopee cushions on your chair and to consider Velcro shoes, as walking out with your shoelaces tied together can be problematic. Why mention this? Because I believe there is a pompousness that can permeate both our industries, an ego-driven attitude the dehumanizes tech and healthcare companies alike, making it more difficult for their employees to empathize and connect with their customers. In a stultifying culture, people are more hesitant to speak truth to power. Fear and hesitation creep in, crimping the spirit of sharing and openness that fosters new ideas. By staying human, by remembering to laugh, we build a stronger company that better serves our clients and members.

Not all ideas are great ideas, but if you play with them, they often grow better and stronger. That's the ideal anyway. But even if the idea dies, a culture that is nurturing and playful still makes people feel safe, so that more ideas show up. People should never feel threatened simply because their idea did not fly. In forbidding corporate cultures, people clam up, worried that their risky notion will mean the end of their career trajectory. So play is important. Critical even and a lot more fun.

## Giving

One aspect of our culture that I think is critical is our focus on giving. We're all about contributing. Pitching in. When someone asks you for something, you give. You don't have to give a lot, but you always give. The fact that a colleague has gone out of their way to ask you to contribute, to support, you find a way to be part of that. Maybe it's a donation, maybe it's volunteering. It's the concept that we're all in this together. Nobody is exempt from it. So helping, whether it be helping a member, helping the community, or helping the company move forward even in a small way, is everyone's responsibility to bring our service to life and make that service effective. As a result of this spirit, we're a company of people working our butts off, with the accelerator always pressed flat to the floor, while simultaneously having a great time. It's about mutual support, generosity of spirit, and an understanding that we're all in it together. As much as any innovation or strategic insight, I believe it is that giving spirit that is responsible for our enjoying a great deal of success in the marketplace.

It's also made clear that it is not how much one gives, but that one gives at all – not just inside the office, but in the outside world as well. We recently raised $5,500 internally, which we dispersed to various members in our organization who were suffering economic hardships, including a member whose house had recently burned down. Since 2015, we have raised $400,000 for the Juvenile Diabetes Research Foundation (JDRF). We also collectively donated to support Team Livongo cyclists riding one hundred miles to raise money for research to find a cure for type 1 diabetes, paying the travel expenses of all employees who participated. For some, the cost of getting the rider to the ride location and shipping their bike, etc., costs more than they raised. So why do this? Community. Team. Commitment. There's no way I can overstate our team's sincere commitment. For instance, summing up a recent JDRF ride in Wisconsin, Livongo team member Andy Devries wrote:

> The bike I rode on was a Schwinn Traveler from the 1980s, and it was one of the least fancy bikes I saw anyone riding that weekend. I felt different from the other riders and was sure I would be uncomfortable and at a disadvantage. I even contemplated upgrading bikes shortly before the race. However, I decided to ride it partly because it's what I bought and had been riding all summer, but also for a more philosophical reason: Having type 1 diabetes is un-

comfortable. It affects your diet, sleep, and activity levels. By the end of the ten-hour ride, my neck hurt, my butt felt as though it was going to fall off, and I had a serious cramp in my hamstring. But after I crossed the finish line, I had a chocolate milk, took a nap, and the next day I felt fine. Having type 1 isn't like that – there's no walking away from it. In riding my old bike, I decided to experience for one day a discomfort symbolic of those who face type 1 diabetes every day.

That provides a pretty awesome snapshot of how our team embraces an inclusive and passionate culture of empathy.

For our holiday outreach, we sent more than four thousand clients, prospects, partners, and other friends of Livongo an email offering them the opportunity to select a charity to which Livongo would make a donation. Always staying mission-focused, we chose three charities that align with the chronic conditions we support as well as the three Cs we address when silencing noisy healthcare:

- American Heart Association (Confusion): Fund innovative research, advocacy, and support to address heart disease and stroke.

- Partnership for a Healthier America (Complexity): Partner with the private sector to make healthier choices, like food and physical activity, and increase demand for these healthier options.

- Insulin for Life (Cost): Provide insulin and glucose-monitoring supplies free of charge to people with diabetes who otherwise might go without them.

# Leadership

One of the opportunities in a growing business is that every day we add someone new. We are continually restarting. Because the composition of the team is now new, this lets each new Livongo member truly have an opportunity to make an impact on the business. I came in less than a year after the team was up and running. And I was able get a snapshot of the organization's culture and help form a narrative on what was working and what wasn't. I was also able to see the strengths of that original core team.

There's no doubt in my mind that eventually some MBA program will try to templatize the leadership skills that have made Glen Tullman such an incredibly successful CEO. There are obviously elements inherent to his personality, as he is naturally whip-smart, a quick study, and has a genius for making others feel incredibly special. He also fosters an environment that people want to be part of – the enthusiasm starts at the top and percolates everywhere. Glen's created an environment where everyone in the company feels responsible for a healthy culture. We take the business very seriously, but we do not take ourselves seriously. Of course, he additionally had a great idea and vision for the actual what of the business, but the thing that impressed me most was the leadership team he built around that vision. His core crew reveals a lot about what ingredients comprise a successful, thriving team.

I remember reading once that the secret to Steven Spielberg's success as a director is not simply his remarkable cinematic vision but, more importantly, his team of professionals – from cinematography to costume to continuity – whom he keeps relatively constant, regardless of the project. He knew who was valuable, whom he trusted, and whom he should bring along from film to film. It created a shorthand, the ability to pass the ball without looking and know a teammate will be there to catch it. (I love basketball. Fun fact: I was starting point guard, number 21, for the Cotter Ramblers, nicknamed "The Road Runner.") We live in an era where the auteur or "great man" idea still permeates society. The hope that a Thomas Edison, a Bill Gates, or an Elon Musk is going to just make greatness happen is a patently false notion. Yes, brilliant, incredible leaders exist. But they're only able to show how incredible they are because of the people they attract and the loyalty, passion, and drive they bring out in the people who surround them.

We currently have a great team and continue to add to it, evolving and changing roles as we grow together. But almost every winning team has a few core anchors driving the momentum toward success. I will mention a few our ours. Not simply because these are great people I deeply respect and look to for inspiration and guidance, but also because they provide archetypes for roles that you often need in start-up companies to be successful.

*Archetype #1: Product Guru*

I don't know if he would appreciate the comparison, but Amar Kendale is the Livongo equivalent of Hermione Granger. He is wicked smart, very insightful, and eagerly helps people around him, sort of like how Hermione lets Harry and Ron copy her homework. He's a bit like the king of archetypes in this role – Apple's Steve Wozniak, an engineer with both clear precision and an incredible amount of empathy. This makes him the perfect person to oversee the development of products that will affect people with chronic conditions. It's inspiring to see the pride he takes when he hears how our products have made a difference in members' lives. A very early member of the team, Amar started in business development (he is a strategic thinker) and transitioned to lead our product, ultimately earning the title of Chief Product Officer. He is adored by his team and has become a powerful, enthusiastic speaker as the external face of Livongo.

Amar is a great example of the principle that you can bring on really smart and talented people who culturally fit and then figure out their best role based on their strengths and our needs. When you start a company, you want to fill your roster with excellent, well-rounded athletes, and as you all mature, you figure out how to make all of them excel in whatever it is that will become their specialty, the expertise that will allow them to play at the top of their game and push the company to a higher level.

*Archetype #2: Sales Mastermind*

Character matters. Jim Pursley, our Chief Commercial Officer, is one of the people you can bet on to do the right thing. Always. It is in his DNA. He is not only a true professional, but a good person. He's our model on how to be a team player, probably because he played football at Penn State. Because of that, he often leverages sports analogies, heroes, and heroics to motivate his team. He is well-liked, hardworking, and one of the people you want in the foxhole with you. He can also do that wonderful thing where he may disagree with a direction and clearly articulate his opinion, then, if another decision is made, be 100% behind whatever is best for the company. He often says, "Experience is what you get when you do not get what you want."

When things are going well, everything is easy. It is when the chips are down that you need to have a team of people you can absolutely, deeply trust. I wasn't around back when Apple was starting up – I was back in Minnesota riding around my yard on a tricycle – but along with Steve Jobs, the mercurial iconoclast, and Woz, the wunderkind programmer, I'm betting that there was a player like Jim, pulling the team together and driving them. I would bet on Jim every day of the week. And twice on Wednesday.

*Archetype #3: The Heart*

This is Joe Carey, initially in the role of Chief Operating Officer. Joe is a seasoned professional with oodles of experience. He is truly the heart of the company. We sometimes joke that "family is everything to Joe, and everyone is family." His true family really is number one, and it has been inspiring to see, in a world where people often ignore their personal responsibilities in pursuit of success, how incredibly professionally successful Joe has been operating under that mantra. He cares about people in a way that inspires incredible trust, which enables him to be perfectly direct; he has no problem voicing his (often) dissenting opinion in a very respectful way.

Joe has shown me that you can build a company with many of the principles of family: Tolerate one another, voice opinions, and embrace respect and difference. As Microsoft CEO Satya Nadella says in his book, *Hit Refresh*:

> Leaders take internal and external noise and synthesize a message from it, recognizing the true signal within a lot of noise. I don't want to hear that someone is the smartest person in the room. I want to hear them take their intelligence and use it to develop deep shared understanding within teams and define a course of action.[3]

Our own company's leadership is a mix of introverts and extroverts, with high EQs, big hearts, gregarious laughs, and a willingness to share a cup of tea with anyone. It's not surprising that people like working with them. But more importantly, in my eyes, this leadership team exemplifies the idea that culture is not something that any one person is responsible for – unless you're a museum or an art school, there should never be a "chief culture officer." Instead, it falls to each of us every day. We live a culture. As a leader, people watch everything you do – what you eat, if you wear earpods or headphones, and especially how you treat people. By embracing and personally embodying empathy, teamwork, and familial trust, the founders of Livongo have set the stage for more than a winning company. They've laid the groundwork for a successful culture.

## Growth and Culture

One key issue that stymies successful companies is how you keep your mojo once the growth kicks in. For us, it's an especially relevant question, because while we are a mission-driven company, with Applied Health Signals and AI+AI in place, we're also a machine. On a single day in 2019 we onboarded more than two hundred clients. It's a lot of work and a ton of growth with a tremendous amount more down the road. How do we keep the same sparkle in the eye and fire in the belly?

Normally, entering other lines of business would dilute a mission, distract people, and more often than not set a company on a path to irrelevance. For us, that ambition is an element that keeps our passion evergreen. By working on the whole person, we are able to continually expand our mission deeper into the human condition, solving more problems, providing more empowerment, enabling more members to live better lives. It's simple. Whether it's diabetes or de-

---

[1] Nadella, Satya. Hit Refresh: The Quest To Rediscover Microsoft's Soul And Imagine A Better Future For Everyone. Harperbusiness, 2017.

pression or back pain, the end result of our work is the same. So instead of dispersing our energy and diluting our message, we're actually strengthening it, bringing more people into the tent, making our story more powerful. Recently we had an event where a Livongo employee shared his personal story as a member of our weight-loss program. It was a pretty brave thing to do, and it showed the evangelical energy behind what we're doing. A lot of the credit for encouraging that kind of honesty and transparency goes to the Chief People Officer at Livongo, Arnnon Geshuri, who is the key promoter and amplifier of our culture.

## *Peripheral Vision*

So far, in 2019, we are hiring about two people every business day. We are investing heavily in finding the right talent, maintaining the culture, and giving our current employees new pathways for advancement. We are putting active learning and development systems in place to get people up to speed and keep them speeding along. One question is, how do we address the practical day-to-day need to drive business results and execute perfectly while still being a visionary company filled with innovation, insights, and the ability to embrace failure? It's virtually impossible to do that in an organization that's onboarding one thousand members every single day, without designing for it.

So we designed for it. We developed an innovation center – Livongo Labs – within our already pretty small, innovative company. Its focus is to keep watch for tech opportunities, harvesting and nurturing creativity from the entire organization, experimenting, and piloting ideas we think might lead to new products, systems, and market breakthroughs. Overall, we're working to capture what McKinsey calls "orthogonal thinking," in which notions from unexpected, unpredictable places can lead to progress. The team also brings together diverse disciplines for hack days, accelerating the ideation process into hyperspeed to see what we can come up with. It might not be as grand as legendary workshops like Bell Labs or Xerox's PARC, yet the principles are the same; it's an environment that touches product, design, data science, clinical, and engineering resources. And Livongo Labs even has its own T-shirt (which is a clear sign that it receives celebratory attention). Most importantly, it's a space that is safe for failure, encourages false starts and dead ends, and lives about as far

away from the sales-results culture that defines the other wing of our company as possible. We need both, and we invest proportionately.

## *Curing the Hiccups*

At the beginning of 2018, it was clear to me that our competitors were all telling the same story we were. We had decided to build and launch our hypertension product, and we needed to differentiate ourselves. We had very quickly developed our new sales material to tell a new story about taking care of the whole person. It framed the issue well and delivered a strong signal to the market, showing a vision and opening a door toward future growth. But the way in which we launched this idea was not nearly as collaborative as it needed to be. I was under a crazy timetable and spent the Christmas break holed up with a marketing lead. Even though it was exactly the right answer, and a perfectly logical one, when we finally unveiled it to the company, it was met with some resistance. Because it wasn't a truly cooperative group effort.

Right away I recognized my errors. I had not managed the change well, especially to a sales team that was out there working hard and experiencing great success selling the diabetes story with our original material. In their eyes, I was trying to fix something that wasn't broken. So, unsurprisingly in retrospect, it fell pretty flat at sales training. But a year later, after seeing my missteps, massaging the story, and taking the time to get the whole team involved, our pivot into the Applied Health Signals positioning has been an early success for us. The lesson, and perhaps it's an obvious one still worth being reminded about, is that a great idea is worthless unless you can get the team invested in it. Making the effort to test notions, language, and approaches with key players on your team early on will make any concept's chance of success that much greater.

To that end, last year, when I knew we needed to share our vision of where we were taking the company and healthcare, I thought of my experience with Play Bigger.

We had worked with Play Bigger when I was at Castlight, a respected category design leader partnering with tech entrepreneurs and executives to help hone, coach, and serve companies as they built their stories. Naomi Allen (whom I had also known from Castlight) was working with Play Bigger when we began discussing a possible collaboration. Ultimately, Play Bigger was simply out of our price range. Our CEO said we couldn't afford it. But for an entrepreneurial company, or any of my three kids, "no" is just the beginning of a conversation. I had to figure out another way. Determined and confident that we needed to share our broader vision with the market, I did the next best creative thing I could think of: I hired Naomi to lead these efforts and other strategic growth initiatives. She had the expertise and all of the right cross-collaboration skills I had missed the first time around. Even further, to truly be successful with a category creation, it takes years of work, constant messaging, product realignment, and company OKRs. To have someone internal, constantly championing what we are doing, gives us a better shot at winning in the long term.

## Building With a Human Touch

We are a human company leveraging technology to empower our members. A key word there is "human." Our coaches are the face of Livongo to our members. They are the ones who create the bond of trust and empathy that makes the entire system work. Because all of us in healthcare will need to interact with a person at some point. The goal is to get the right person at the right point on the right topic.

We have coaches, but we do not use call centers. Our team of one hundred coaches (and growing every day) are all direct employees of Livongo, each one a highly trained practitioner. They have thousands of hours of education and training and years of experience as Certified Diabetes Educators (CDEs), RNs, LPNs, Licensed Dietitian Nutritionists (LDNs), Registered Dietitian Nutritionists (RDNs), Exercise Physiologists (EPs), and every combination of these degrees and disciplines, among others. They are already really impressive professionals in their own fields, but that doesn't mean they have the entire knowledge base they necessarily need across all disciplines.

To effectively empower our members to get healthier and transform their lives, we need to break down the silos of specialization in healthcare and cross-train our coaches for all conditions. We train so they can deliver expertise across a broad spectrum of disciplines, whether it be diabetes care, exercise, nutrition, high blood pressure, medication, or helping members deal with stress. And then we provide them with a full electronic picture of every member they are talking with, so every conversation is informed, intimate, and familiar.

From a business perspective, in an industry where everything is digitized, having a human element like our coaches is increasingly unusual. Consumers are perfectly comfortable with service industries that are entirely automated. Think about how rarely you have ever spoken to a customer-service representative at Amazon or eBay. Do they even exist? Working with real people is also expensive, which is why Uber is driving the research on autonomous cars and why supermarkets are investing in automated checkout. The difference with Livongo is that, for us, having some kind of human connection is critical. It is critical because this is healthcare. We believe that every person in the healthcare system at some point in their journey will not just want but need to interact with another person. Not all the time, but at a distinct time. As Lee Shapiro (the one who encouraged Glen to start Livongo in the first place) says, "Tech without touch doesn't hunt in health."

> ● ● ●
> **Not coaching supported by digital. It is digital to enable really, really smart coaching.**
> ● ● ●

Which leads to a challenging question: How do we manage this resource alongside our rapid growth? As our programs and offerings expand, one could imagine call centers as big as football fields, with payroll budgets and costs soaring. The answer lies in our technology itself. And the beauty is in the iteration column of AI+AI.

By continuously A/B testing messaging, texts, alerts, and Health Nudges, we know (and never stop learning) what works and what doesn't for each and every person, condition, and circumstance. This enables us to do what all the coaches in the world couldn't do alone at our scope – to anticipate and respond appropriately and effectively in real time at just the right time for all our members in the right way. Everyone is coached digitally first, then matched with a human resource to drive to the greatest outcomes, when they want it or need it (for instance, when they are having a dangerously low blood sugar reading and want assurance they are not alone). This is the key to Livongo's scalability. It is not coaching supported by digital. It is digital to enable really, really smart coaching.

Alongside that, of course, we will be also adding new services, addressing other chronic conditions, and finding better ways to empower people. So the role will always be there for the coaches. They are our empathy engine by working in tandem with digital. And the flywheel learning allows us to evolve our offering so that every interaction is more targeted, more valuable, and more effective.

## *Working With Providers*

Providers, given their power to write prescriptions, are key stakeholders in this new ecosystem we've created. And we are now developing relationships with the most innovative health systems in the country, like Jefferson Health, led by the visionary Dr. Stephen Klasko. Organizations that recognize the new role and potential of the empowered healthcare consumer, that recognize they are in the service industry, have discovered how Livongo can help.

Robin Sheldon, Senior Vice President for strategic planning ventures at Jefferson Health, looks at Livongo in a couple different ways:

I really think it's amazing how Livongo is always trying to figure out what the data means and how best to consume it. That's a really big issue for us as a health system, too, because it's not about "data, data, data." It's about a kind of smart data, and what you do with the data, and how meaningful the data is. People sometimes lose sight of that, and Livongo hasn't.

A large part of Robin's focus at Jefferson is innovation with out-side companies like Livongo, looking to help improve products and services in ways that would benefit Jefferson and the people it serves. Robin and her team first discovered Livongo when Jefferson Health merged with another health system. "One of the things that we noticed when we were doing all of our due diligence was this wonderful tool. Then we dug into what it was that Livongo was offering, had some discussions, and then that led to an even deeper relationship."

A critical part of our success is avoiding the arrogance that often comes from working in tech, especially in Silicon Valley, and being open to collaboration. Robin and her team made suggestions to our platform early on, proposing new ways to increase the ease of physi-cian engagement. Robin explains it this way:

> Our relationship with Livongo started as a rather standard vendor/vendee – we were a very early customer. So, yes, our employees and beneficiaries get the Livongo glucose meter and coaching as an employee benefit, but that's not the extent of our relationship. We're also collaborating with them to develop different aspects of their products, their financial models, and ideas for new products and services.

It will be collaborations like the work we've done with Jefferson that will lead to our ultimate success with healthcare providers. As that industry awakens to the empowered healthcare consumer, we believe the work we have already done together with innovation leaders like Jefferson will make the evolution of our industry just that much easier.

## *Chapter Fifteen Summary: Betting on the Culture*

- Change in healthcare is not likely to come from doctors and healthcare administrators but from other varied disciplines – with diversity in experience, thinking, and point of view.

- Changing (and improving) the system starts with a great team. It takes a special mix of people with a wide range of talents. Just like our product offerings, our hiring balances both IQ and EQ.

- Promote a healthy culture. Embrace play. Focus on giving. Invest in talent.

- A great team creates scalable success.
  - On a single day in 2019 we onboarded more than two hundred clients.
  - We onboard more than one thousand new members every single day.
  - We are hiring about two people every business day in 2019.
  - Our coaches are highly trained practitioners from a multitude of professions and disciplines who are then further trained in coaching fundamentals and empathetic listening.
  - We have great collaborative partnerships in place and will continue to extend into the provider world to acheive better results and a fully integrated experience for our members and the physicians who serve them.

# CHAPTER 16

# *What's to Come*

THE TOOLS ARE IN PLACE for our success, and now it is about flawless execution and scaling to offer Livongo to more people every day. The flywheel of AI+AI will only live up to its promise if we look at the data objectively and follow a logical, customer-focused decision tree to deliver services that members value. This is where the foundational work we have done building a reputation and a culture of trust and mutual respect all comes together. It's one thing to build a machine, it's another thing to run it well for the benefit of our members.

At a certain point, too, Livongo will not be thought of as an "add-on" to health plans, but a part of the essential offerings woven into the fabric of the benefits offered to employers and their employees. That has grown to become one of our key objectives: to make Livongo part of the core benefits offered. The idea of disconnecting from Livongo will begin to seem as absurd as deleting an email account with all your contacts' information and addresses, just to start over somewhere else. Yesterday, no one would wonder why Livongo wasn't in their benefits package, but we are already hearing – anecdotally – of employees who are literally checking to see if their employer offers us.

## *Expanding the Platform*

Our work around the whole person began by addressing conditions adjacent to or related to diabetes, like hypertension. Then, after acquiring Retrofit, we were able to expand into both a full diabetes-prevention program and a weight-management program. So now, instead of just talking to one aspect of one condition, we were comprehensively connecting with a broad array of conditions. Then, in January 2019, the purchase of myStrength gave us expertise in behavioral health, from the leader in the space. As we progress, we will consider expanding into other conditions: respiratory health and musculoskeletal issues (hip, back, and knee pain).

But even more than covering new chronic conditions, we are expanding the features that we deliver to each individual, such as medication optimization, which improves health outcomes by addressing medication appropriateness, effectiveness, adherence, and access – a deep, data-driven way to discover what works for an individual and what does not.

If you think about this from a client and member perspective, ultimately we are providing the simplest and most convenient solution possible. Instead of à la carte shopping for all of these conditions, we are the one place they can connect with standardized and optimized service and assistance. We don't just remove the three Cs for diabetes, we eliminate them across the board.

## *Technology + People: Moving Forward*

If you think about how the United Kingdom's National Health

Service runs, it evaluates any given medical intervention with a broad cost-effectiveness analysis. First, it determines if the specific clinical outcome is worth the expenditure at all. It then sets a threshold for what it deems acceptable to spend for a Quality-Adjusted Life Year (the "cost per QALY," as it is known). Medicines and treatments above that limit are unlikely to be recommended, while those that meet the criteria are made available to eligible patients.

Imagine, instead of looking at the societal level, we used technology to run a cost-effectiveness analysis at the *individual* level, so that we could apply the interventions that drive the most valuable outcomes for that individual person. And then we could create a curated marketplace, whereby each individual was offered only those options, whether they be an insulin-dosing algorithm or at-home meal delivery, not only maximizing cost effectiveness, but facilitating a completely positive member experience. That member experience is every bit as valuable to the model as cost savings.

To that end, we believe that in order to solve the crisis with chronic conditions, we must drive to a scalable solution that is both personalized and cost-effective. More care delivered more cost-effectively rather than an unnecessary and painful trade-off. So we will always start with digital coaching and continue to build out care-provider networks that are immediately and easily accessed when people most need to talk with an actual human.

When I joined Livongo, the concept of curating the marketplace was just a glimmer in our eye. How do you get people to actually enroll in the optimal choices? First, we have to understand how to motivate people – with what words, and at what time. In order to do *both*, we needed data scientists, behavior scientists, and health economists to start tracking and measuring what we were doing in real time.

Early on, I asked to build a data science team and I got this response: "Great, get data people to tell us if our solution is working." That was true, but we also needed to invest in data scientists far beyond this, because they were the ingredient that was going to make the product work.

Think about it this way. Manufacturing is ultimately about quality, and so quality control lives at every point of the manufacturing process. Healthcare is an information business. Therefore, we need data science across every level of what we do – from recruitment and enrollment to the specific interventions that drive and maximize outcomes. Every single item in our funnel requires our AI+AI engine. This is how you make an information business function. Without it, all you have is useless piles of data, with no optimization, no innovation.

In Silicon Valley, these people are very expensive. Few companies (especially at our stage) invest in the resources the way they should. Which is why so many companies fail to leverage anything out of the enormous volumes of big data to which they have access. If you don't invest, all that data becomes an unimaginably large haystack and there's no hope of finding any needle. Insights and opportunities are lost. But Livongo's leadership saw the vision and made the necessary hires who would ultimately make all the difference.

We are continuing to invest in earning trust and loyalty, and we are creating a marketplace of sorts to actually serve up curated choices designed for our members. By delivering exactly what each member needs, when they need it, and inspiring enough trust along the way, we will continue to delight with exceptional experiences, deliver measurable clinical outcomes, and rid the system of inefficiency, waste, and noise, which translates into savings. Only in this way can we serve both our members and our clients.

As one of our clients, Hassan Azar, Senior Vice President of total rewards at U.S. Foods, said of Livongo:

Livongo is focused on access and improved access to health-care and data, getting people healthier and then controlling costs. That's their triple-aim, which is very aligned with my triple-aim and my goal. It's putting not only the patient but the people writing the check to pay for healthcare at the center. Making sure that we're all being taken care of. There are medical providers out there that would rather just keep churning and billing and finding new ways to get money out of the system regardless of cost to quality or outcomes. Livongo's purpose is to really empower individuals.

It really democratizes what we offer our employees. They don't have to be living in downtown Chicago or New York City. It's helping all of our employees wherever they are. That's the beauty of a digital solution. It can be everywhere.

As we continue to build and deepen the trust our members have in Livongo, we can continue developing an open application marketplace that allows third-party partners like digital medications, outside coaching solutions, and devices (Apple Watch, home health, smartphone, Siri, smart speakers, etc.) to be connected to the solution in a highly secure manner via standard APIs in order to provide the best applications to Livongo members based on their specific needs. This is taking curated choice to an even higher level. Think of it as a smart app store, with tools we know will help always available and easily accessible.

## *Taking on the Big Stuff*

We believe the difference between a good company and a great company is that a great company makes a real difference. Today, we are a good company. And we are hard at work at becoming a great company. To us, that means doing the right thing, being on the right side of history. Addressing real issues such as insulin affordability: The price of insulin more than tripled between 2002 and 2013 and continues to rise. A 2018 Yale study found that as a grave consequence, "One in four (diabetes) patients admitted to cutting back on insulin use because of cost."[1] It's a problem we're passionately working on right now, and one we believe can be fixed.

People talk about work-life balance. Our passion for important work and our lives at home intersect, overlap. And it has to. Diabetes and other chronic conditions do not turn on and turn off. So it is no surprise that Glen serves on the board of the American Diabetes Association, and the Juvenile Diabetes Research Foundation working on insulin affordability behind the scenes. At the time of the publication of this book, two asks are being explored and discussed: 1) ways to supply insulin at cost from manufacturers with no copays, rebates, handling, or administration fees, and 2) ways to encourage people using the drug to commit to basic monitoring and reporting (so that taking the drug can be verified, eliminating the possibilities of resale).

• • •

**Philanthropy — a responsibility that we believe must be taught, encouraged, and practiced regularly.**

• • •

The program in development is for life-saving insulin only. The ultimate goal is to reduce the cost and increase the availability of insulin to underresourced and underserved populations of people with diabetes.

At Livongo, we are also looking at ways to cover people who have no healthcare coverage. Looking at how we raise and give money to our

---

[1] (Nadella, 2017)

members facing their own economic difficulties. We're also examining how to best empower our philanthropy – a responsibility we believe must be taught, encouraged, and practiced regularly. We know that making healthcare more affordable for everyone makes more dollars available for the underresourced and underserved.

Livongo will continue to lead on this issue, in any and every way we can. Our staff knows the scale and cost of this tenet. We see it in our work and feel it in our lives. As a mission-driven company, issues like these – problems and policies that sit at the core of what so many of our members are forced to endure – are what we must lean into, and never run away from.

## *The Road Ahead*

Robin Sheldon from Jefferson puts it correctly when she says, "The people that need Livongo most right now don't really have access to it."

We have a long way to go.

For the short term, we have to provide a level of service and experience you would expect at Nordstrom or a Four Seasons to all the large companies that are our current clients and, even more importantly, to the employees with the chronic conditions who are our members. We have to exceed their expectations and continue to offer them more, empowering the whole person with a service they love, that makes them healthier and happier, and that costs less or, ideally, is free.

But we are not doing this work simply to make sure the biggest companies have the best health services. We want to be here for everyone. It's been almost ten years since Obamacare changed the healthcare landscape in the United States and made it possible for almost seven million people to become health consumers, making them as empowered in our field as they are in every other service industry. It takes a while to move an industry of this big size, so it's only today that the average healthcare company and consumer are even really beginning to understand how to make the most of these changes.

Our work with the large, self-insured employers provides a great foundation for Livongo's greater ambitions in that they already give us a window to the world. They operate around the world with employees who stand to benefit from our services, and in seeking to empower them, we are beginning to gain a keen understanding of the nuances and complexities of the health category globally. Meanwhile, locally, we're working to increase access to make our solutions accessible to as many people as possible.

All these pieces point to a potent fact: Livongo is approaching a tipping point, where the greater market – national healthcare companies, global industries, world governments, and not least of all, empowered healthcare consumers – will awaken to the possibilities that technology and information have now provided us with a gift that is almost unimaginable: the ability to address the epidemic of chronic conditions – the largest healthcare problem we have ever faced. They will see the power of Applied Health Signals and the dynamic strength of AI+AI when it is in action, helping people get the right information they need at exactly the right time. After that, it will be a question of how nimbly we can scale up, how we balance the human touch with the technology-driven solutions, and how we make empathy work at a truly global scale. It is an enormous task and a daunting challenge. But then I think of everything I have faced ever since that day when I was a little girl sitting in that doctor's office in Minnesota just hearing that she had diabetes. I see everything I have been able to overcome since then. After that, helping the world doesn't seem like some impossible or insurmountable task. It's just one more thing we have to do. Together.

141

# *Chapter Sixteen Summary: What's to Come*

- The only way we will win in the long term is if our members feel as if we are truly there for them.
  - Through the flywheel of AI+AI we will get to know and serve the customer better, in a more personalized and tailored fashion, making it increasingly difficult for a competitor to gain traction.
  - The consumer will drive our momentum. Livongo will not be thought of as an "add-on" to health plans but as part of the fabric of the benefits offered to employers and their members.
  - One of our key objectives is to make Livongo part of the core benefits offered through a health plan across all segments and lines of business.

- We have broadened our platform, moving from diabetes to hypertension, weight management (acquiring Retrofit), diabetes prevention, and behavioral health (acquiring myStrength). We will soon expand to respiratory health and musculoskeletal issues – hip, back, and knee pain. We are also deep-diving into medication optimization.

- Delivering exactly what each member needs, when they need it, and inspiring enough loyalty along the way, we will continue to delight with exceptional experiences, deliver clinical outcomes, and drive inefficiency and waste out of the system.

- As a mission-driven company, issues, problems, and policies that sit at the core of what so many of our members are forced to endure are what we must lean into, and never run away from. Insulin affordability and greater accessibility are at the forefront.

- Livongo is approaching a tipping point, where the greater market – the national healthcare companies, the global industries and governments, the empowered healthcare consumers – will all awaken to the possibilities that technology and information have given us to help cope with the full range of chronic conditions.

# About the Author

DR. JENNIFER SCHNEIDER is the President of Livongo Health. She is responsible for the company's strategic vision, product, data science, engineering, marketing, growth, and clinical operations. She is a frequent speaker about innovation in healthcare, sharing her unique perspective as a physician, health-services researcher, and senior executive. Previously, Dr. Schneider served as Livongo's first Chief Medical Officer for three and a half years.

Prior to Livongo, Dr. Schneider held several key leadership roles at Castlight Health, including in clinical product development and strategic analytics and most recently as Chief Medical Officer. She has also held leadership roles in the provider setting as a health-outcomes researcher and Chief Resident at Stanford University and has practiced medicine as an attending physician at Stanford University, the VA Palo Alto Health Care System, and Kaiser Permanente. Dr. Schneider holds an undergraduate degree from the College of the Holy Cross, an M.D. from Johns Hopkins School of Medicine, and a Master's of Science in health services research from Stanford

University. She completed her internal medicine residency at Stanford University Hospital.

Jenny is an avid athlete who recently completed her first Ironman and has lived with type 1 diabetes for more than thirty years. She has accomplished much, but she is most proud of her children: Fiona, Piper, and Angus. Her goal at Livongo is to create a system of health and healthcare that they will inherit and be proud of. And she hopes they know that, when she is away from them, she's doing work that makes a difference.